CHRISTIANITY

DEMOCRACY AND TECHNOLOGY

CHRISTIANITY

DEMOCRACY AND TECHNOLOGY

by

Zoltan Sztankay

PHILOSOPHICAL LIBRARY
New York

TO THE MEMORY OF MY FATHER

AS THIS BOOK GOES TO THE PRINTER THE MASS-UPRISING OF THE HUNGARIAN PEOPLE FOR FREEDOM IS BEING CRUSHED BY SOVIET STEEL AND FIRE. DAUGHTERS AND SONS OF HUNGARY'S WORKERS AND PEASANTS ARE CONSCIOUSLY GIVING THEIR YOUNG LIVES IN A SUPREME EF-FORT OF SELF-SACRIFICE TO GAIN FREE-DOM.

A PEOPLE OF CHRISTIAN TRADITION IS BEING MARTYRED FOR THEIR BELIEF IN DEMOCRACY. THEY ARE SLAUGHTERED ON THE ORDER OF MEN WHO RIDICULE CHRISTIANITY AND HOLD DEMOCRACY IN CONTEMPT. SOVIET ARMOR AND FIRE-POWER, PRODUCT OF MISUSED TECHNOLOGY, IS SLOWLY CRUSHING THE LIFE OUT OF AN UNARMED PEOPLE WHO WANTED TO LIVE FREE.

WE SOLEMNLY BOW OUR HEADS IN MEMORY OF THOSE WHO DIED FOR OUR FREEDOM AS WELL AS FOR THEIR OWN.

CONTENTS

PART THREE

Chapter V DANGERS OF A TECHNOLOGICAL AGE

PERSONAL NOTE TO THE READER.

I just came back from a stroll through the nearby fields, meadows, and woods. I saw spring arriving. I saw the buds on the old oak trees. I saw the grass turning green. In the haze of the far horizon I saw patches of light green on the hillside as a witness to the germination of last fall's sowing. The skies are blue and the wind is blowing from the south. There is warmth in the air. Birds fly high and their song of freedom fills my heart with joy. The whistle of a passing train is piercing the atmosphere.

I feel myself a part of this solemn spectacle which makes me radiantly happy. The irrepressible forces of the returning spring sweep through all my senses. I am overwhelmed by the power of the yearly recreation unfolding before my eyes. In the setting of this triumphant symphony of nature's renewal all worries leave me. I feel as light and happy as a child; I see life once more winning over death. All fears vanish. I realize anew that man never will be able to destroy life. He never will be able to destroy himself. Life is divine. Man never will be able to overcome God.

Under the influence of this inspiration I turn to my past. Europe with both its sins and glories is behind me. I am a son of Europe, the continent which gave so much to mankind and also took away so much; where Christian civilization grew and where democracy arose; where technology was born. I owe so much to Europe. Life, youth, love, poetry, literature, knowledge, faith—all came to me in Europe. My past reposes in Europe.

I came from a part of Europe where East and West meet. I came from the borderland between the two. In the course of long centuries the people of Central-Eastern Europe fought the invaders from the East. They defended the West and the rising Christian culture. Hungarians, Slavs, Balts, Austrians, and Rumanians died by the millions on the battlefields so that Christian Europe should survive. They went down together under the pressure of the last surge of Eastern anti-Christianism. Western man still has to recognize his debt to Eastern Europe. In tribute to those who suffer and gain no recognition, I offer my gratitude to all its peoples. Recalling the faded memories of my childhood, I acknowledge that my native Hungary was very good to me.

In this atmosphere of spring and hope I turn back to the present. For me the present is the new world of the United States. I am an adopted son of this great country. I chose this land to be my own because I believe in the ideals it stands for. I made this choice voluntarily. I willed to become an American. Not the mere chance of birth made me one. I have already made the choice which mankind still has to make. I lived in the Bolshevik-communist part of the world where I could have stayed. Knowingly, willingly, deliberately I chose the West, the United States. I decided for the ideals which this nation symbolizes for me: Christian faith and democratic politics. I preferred progress. With my eyes wide open to the choice which mankind is still facing, I escaped the false promise of an earthly paradise. I refused to believe in the enslaving, man-made doctrines.

I owe so much to this country and to its people. I have faith in my own and man's future because I believe in the ideals which this nation upholds. I am deeply convinced that salvation from the earthly ills of mankind can come only if this nation will live up to its high mission. I have strong faith that this people will stay loyal to its Christian-democratic heritage. An end to the present predicament of mankind can come only if the United States will lead the world in the right direction, namely of human co-operation. However, I am not without fear and doubt. Not everything is right in America. Material temptations are too strong. Defection from Christian principles is a deadly danger likewise here.

I owe my own freedom and that of my family, my own life and that of my family, to the United States. This country accepted us as refugees. It feeds and shelters us.

Finally I turn my vision towards a coming world: the future of mankind. I owe ultimately everything to God. No man, no people, no nation can have a future of its own all by itself. All people of the world are essential members of the human race. There is only one future from now on, the future of mankind. I am a man, an individual human being, but I feel that I am a part of the whole human race: thus I am brother to every man, white, brown, black, or yellow. Wherever a human being is in trouble, I feel his trouble. Wherever a human being of any color is debased, I am debased. Wherever a child is hungry, I am hungry. Wherever a human being is humiliated, I am humiliated. I lift my vision to the future of man. I am thinking about the possibility of human reunification. I wrote this book because I am a part of the essential whole, because I am part of mankind.

* * *

There are also particular statements of gratitude I wish to make. The inspiration for this book came from Dr. O. P. Kretzmann, President of Valparaiso University. It never would have been written and never could have been published without his encouragement and support. It is indeed an honor to recognize his inspiration, advice, and guidance.

Several of my colleagues on the faculty of Valparaiso University were kind enough to read the manuscript in whole or in part. Among them I owe most to Professor John H. Strietelmeier, Managing Editor of The Cresset, who from an early stage of this venture so generously gave his counsel and editorial suggestions. I am also much indebted to Dr. Herbert Umbach, who was kind enough to correct part of the manuscript and advise me on many relevant details. I recognize the assistance of Mr. Sherman Johnsrud, who offered suggestions about the form of the manuscript. I acknowledge the clerical help I received from Mrs. Palmer Czamanske, who was kind enough to do the typing of the manuscript.

To write a book is often an agonizing work. The strain of the job sorely tests one's endurance and nerves. I never could have completed the task without the loving encouragement and assistance of my wife. Actually my wife and our son contributed considerably to the correction of the final product.

Z. S.

PART ONE

PART ONE

CHAPTER I

THE WORLD TODAY

1. INTERNATIONAL INTERDEPENDENCE BUT NO ORGANIZATION

By modern science man has transformed the world. Modern man prides himself on having enslaved the forces of nature and even on becoming the master of his own destiny. He sets his eyes upon the highest goal: he wants to become secure, prosperous, and free.

Yet, wherever we look man trembles with fear at the possibility of a Third World War in a time when war very well might bring an end to our civilization as we know it today.

Man now has the means to bring about prosperity over the whole world as it has already been done in the United States. Yet, by far the greater portion of mankind is living in misery. Many hundred millions of our fellowmen daily live with the problem of keeping body and soul together.

Political democracy has become a fact in most of the Western countries and individual freedoms are there respected. However, totalitarian governments are ruling well over one-third of the globe's population, and freedom is trying to gain a precarious foothold in the rest of the world. Western democracy itself is in danger.

We, in this country, are beginning to feel that these plights of the rest of the world are our own. The First World War was fought to end all wars and establish permanent peace all over the world. The Second World War was a great enough blow to knock out all the illusions about isolationism from American heads and to deflate the idea that this country can have peace while the rest of the world is at war.

1

Intelligent Americans have no illusions that our political democracy could survive if the rest of the world is taken over by totalitarian dictatorships. Some people in this country still remember one of the slogans under which the nation fought in the First World War: to make the world safe for democracy. Even more must recall that the United States became involved in the Second World War in order to stop the fascist dictators from conquering the world and to prevent them from extinguishing human rights and freedoms. The situation has not changed since then. We are fighting the cold war because our political democracy and our civil liberties are endangered by outside forces.

While this country's dependence on foreign nations in the economic sense was the first to be understood by the experts, I wonder if the average American well understands how insecure our exceptional prosperity is and how much it depends on the rest of the world. Prosperous America is living on borrowed time. Happily, ever since the end of the Second World War those responsible for our government are well aware of this fact. Otherwise they would not have spent many billions of dollars to help foreign nations gain a better life.

All these facts indicate that the nations of the world have become dependent on each other. A relatively new word is used more and more by the experts and has found acceptance by the laymen, namely "interdependence." Yes, the word interdependence, as applied to the relations of all nations, has become one of the most used in the textbooks on international relations. International interdependence is not only an abstract textbook expression. International interdependence is very much a reality. It is a fact. It is a most important factual situation which slowly grew into what it is today.

The complex problem of international interdependence (as we have seen before) has several implications. In order to make this problem of international interdependence clearly understood, it would be helpful to deal with the different aspects of the same problem separately. However, while we are dealing with the different aspects of interdependence separately we are doing this only for the purpose of study. We do not mean to imply that the practical fact of international in-

2

terdependence could also be classified in separate categories corresponding to the several theoretical aspects of the same problem. In practice international interdependence is an indivisible whole.

Let us then first deal with the economic aspects of this problem of interdependence.

International economic interdependence was brought about by man's action, but it was not intended or planned by him. The process which led to the present intensity of economic interdependence of all nations started as a consequence of the industrial revolution at the end of the eighteenth century.

Since the industrial revolution, Western man has built ever-improving means and instruments of communication and transportation. With the help of modern communication the opening of the rest of the world was accelerated beyond imagination. At the same time industrialization of the West began. It was made possible by new technical inventions which in turn were based on some of the basic laws of physics proclaimed by great physicists of earlier centuries, such as Copernicus, Kepler, Galileo, and Newton. The application of the laws of physics was not less brilliant. Practical discoveries followed each other in quick succession. Soon came their early industrial application. During the advancing nineteenth century, ever-increasing numbers of industrial factories were built. Their products were sold not only on the domestic but also on foreign markets. As the market for industrial products grew, the need of raw materials also kept growing. New fields of important minerals were discovered in the faraway lands of Asia and Africa. Growing industries needed new markets and the great European powers became engaged in acquiring colonies and in building immense empires. The natural wealth of the overseas territories in industrial raw materials was too great a temptation for the captains of industry to resist. New industries based on imported raw materials were established. Contemporary researchers in the field of natural sciences came out with new inventions which industry was quick to put to practical use. New industrial articles appeared on the market which by this time had far outgrown the home consumption. Industries in the western countries began to depend more and more on foreign markets. The world market gradually became a reality.

In this process of industrialization the economic structure of the western states was wholly transformed. Agriculture was pushed into second rank. Industrialization was sought and energetically pursued. Great trading and manufacturing cities were built. The population of these metropolitan centers kept on swelling as many persons left the farmlands and joined in greater and greater numbers the ranks of the industrial working class. The growing population needed to be fed. Along with the import of industrial raw materials, European countries became more and more dependent on shipping food from overseas to feed their population. They became dependent on the less developed territories of the world for raw materials, food, and markets for their products.

A parallel process of bringing a change in the economic structure of the dependent colonies went on at the same time. The Asians and the Africans gradually had to give up their exclusive dependence on subsistence agriculture. Many millions of them were put on the plantations to grow the needed raw materials for their Western masters. Natives were also needed for the exploitation of the newly discovered mines and for manning the means of transportation and the handling of trade and other services. For good or bad the needs of the natives are even now becoming more complex. To satisfy these requirements, they depend on the industries of the West. As growers and exporters of raw materials their dependence on the West is even more compelling. They might not be happy with their new way of life, but they are resolved not to go back to subsistence agriculture.

In this process of developing world trade, great modern ports, metropolitan cities, new railroads, and highways were built by international capital all over the world. Export and import trade became vital for all nations.

Industrial countries started to specialize among themselves, as England did in producing the choicest of woolen goods, and their mutual trade contributed further to their respective interdependence.

Today we talk about the world market—and there certainly is one. The prices of the raw materials, food, and industrial products are influenced by the aggregate of world production of each particular article. We talk about the world price of cotton, wool, copper, or about the world price of industrial articles. World trade is intercommunicative and prices are set by world competition. They are quoted at the great commodity markets of the world. The finances of all countries are also part of a single system which is world-wide as the value of each national currency is influenced by its quotation on the world money market. Banking is international and so is shipping. International air-lines are spanning the whole globe. We certainly would have an international labor market if most of the states did not close their borders to immigration or control its flow. The United States built up its great population and acquired its present fine labor force because of the fact that poorly paid European labor moved in the direction of high wages. Today we can truly say that through this economic transformation the world has become a single economic unit with national economic units depending on each other.

The process of making the nations economically dependent on each other started and was carried out without any planning by the states involved. Private initiative, hunger for profit, did the trick. Even in our days, when international economic interdependence is one of the most important facts, this interlinking structure of world economy remains without any regulating central authority. The whole system, so to say, is self-regulating.

Here is one danger. While this complex system of interdependent world economy is in its international aspects only self-regulating, it is nonetheless very real. It is real in the sense that not only the fate of the component national economic units, but the state of the whole human race depend on it. For good or bad the world has become a thoroughly interdependent economic unit. To give one example, the living standard in each country is determined by the role which that country plays in the world economy (industrial territories have higher living standards). Thus the economic well-being of the individual citizens is not exclusively in the hands of their respective governments. A nation's economy

5

can be vitally affected by occurrences abroad. As the complex world economy is only self-regulating, lacking central control and central planning, economic disaster might hit at any component national economy and spread all over the world at any time. The calamity of world depression is ever close at hand.

This important fact of international economic interdependence not only ties the nations of the world into a closely knit economic unit; it has many other, not economic, consequences. We want to examine only its effect on the population problem of the world. An interdependent world economy makes a considerably greater world population possible. Many more hundred millions were born and many more millions stayed alive and lived longer because of all the new opportunities offered as the consequence of an interdependent international economy and because of the much higher living standard made possible by it. Since the beginning of the industrial revolution, which started the process leading to economic interdependence of the nations, the population of the world has doubled or increased even more.

Here lies also a warning. Only this complex, interdependent world economy of ours can support the present very dense and fast-growing population of the world. If the present connections of the local national economies should be severed, if each of them (or even if only a group of them) should fall back to its own sphere and try to depend on its own potentials, we would have a surplus population in the world amounting possibly, let us say, to more than several hundred millions of human beings. This would bring danger not only in the sense that all people would have to lower their living standard very sharply, but indeed many millions could not be fed at all. Without our complex industry and mechanized agriculture, both of which depend on the interdependent world economy, the world could not feed the surplus population.

In consequence of the severance of economic relations among nations, the whole economic structure everywhere would come tumbling down. Misery would overcome uncountable millions. There would be mass starvation, especially in metropolitan cities. Those who would survive this cata-

6

clysm's impact on human life would have to go back to the most primitive type of subsistence agriculture. It is beyond our imagination to picture all the resulting miseries. The more industrialized and progressive a country is, the more it would have to suffer from the terrible consequences of such a disaster. The backward nations of Asia and Africa are less dependent on foreign trade. For them the change back to subsistence agriculture would not involve such difference in the way of life and in their living standard as it would for the industrialized nations. It would not involve so much suffering there as it would in the western industrialized countries.

When we think of the interdependence linking together the nations of the world in an as yet insufficiently appreciated community of interest, we usually have in mind the economic interdependence of the world. This is the reason why we dealt first with the economic implications of international interdependence. However, as we have already stated, the problem has also other aspects. Next, let us take a look at the security aspect of this problem.

The nations of the world are dependent on each other for the maintenance of their security, which means the security of all of their citizens. In other words, the problem of war and peace is common to all the nations. We can talk about the interdependence of the security of all nations. The problem of peace defies solution unless all the nation states recognize it as the most vital and the most urgent question common to them all and unite in an effort to lay the foundation of permanent peace.

Modern communication and transportation completely transformed geographical relations between states. Distance lost much of its hindering effect on communication and transportation. Measured in time, both travel and transportation between the same two geographical points has been reduced from months to days and from weeks to hours. This was indeed a happy development, but the military implications of this tremendous change are sinister in an easily intercommunicable globe, especially in an age of super weapons.

As a result of man's victory over distance and over the amount of time needed for travel, the globe has become a

7

small place to live in. It can be likened to a neighborhood of nations. In terms of air travel and transportation, the nations have all become neighbors indeed. This can be all right. However, these neighbors are quarrelsome and do not recognize law among themselves. They do not feel themselves bound by international morality. They have no court (in the real sense of the word) to submit their disputes to. Neither have they proper organization to guarantee their peace. The individual states that make up the neighborhood have a tendency to take the law into their own hands.

On account of the changed geographical relations between the nation-states and also because of the new superweapons, any unscrupulous power (properly prepared) can easily hit at any of his distant fellow-states and knock out its defences in a matter of days or even hours. Not only is every country of the globe open to attacking airplanes of any other country, but man already possesses ballistic missiles able to fly over the air space of the neutrals and all intervening oceans or even to hit at the target through the exosphere with devastating effect. In the military sense each nation has become the next-door neighbor of any other nation. The security of each nation has become, in this sinister sense, interdependent.

Nor is this the whole meaning of international interdependence. Beyond economic and security implications, interdependence among nations also has ideological and political ramifications. With good reasons we fear for our free political institutions. Our freedom can also be endangered from outside. Our democracy hardly could survive the collapse of like institutions in the rest of the presently free world. The maintenance of our freedom depends thus on factors which originate abroad. In an interdependent world our freedom, too, depends on how the free institutions fare and how they develop in the rest of the world.

The overwhelming majority of mankind is still living in destitution, caused partly by neglect and partly by injustice. The poor and the misery-ridden peoples of the world are above all interested in the improvement of their material conditions. They do not take their misery for granted any more. They are destitute but they are not ignorant. They are

8

searching for the cause of their plight. They want to find the solution of their greatest problem: backwardness and resultant misery. They compare the situation as it is at home with that abroad. They know the difference between the West and East. The daily press, the radio, and the different media of propaganda help to stir up people's interest everywhere, even among nomads, in world affairs and in conditions prevailing abroad.

The people of Asia and Africa feel that they too are entitled to a better life. Their own leaders and the Communist agents are telling them that all nations are responsible for the well-being of each other. They take it for granted that the advanced nations should assist the less fortunate ones. They are convinced that human misery could be altogether eradicated from the face of the earth if only *all* nations, no matter whether rich or poor, would co-operate to attain this aim. They sense that international organization, law, and long-range planning could lead to success. They are determined to have a better life. World-wide solutions are offered to them. Their eagerness to attain a higher standard of life might induce them to listen to the advocates of false promises or even make them accept easy but false solutions. In such manner the cold war is fought in terms of political and economic ideologies.

The agitators and fanatics are not only telling them that the rich are responsible for the poor; they also put the blame on "evil" political and economic institutions as the cause of all human misery. They are blaming the political and economic institutions of the West for the troubles of the world. The poor and the desperate are made to believe that once they accept a certain ideology their misfortune will be over. More than one-third of the population of the world is indoctrinated, from a very tender age on, with the teachings of Karl Marx. Another one-third or more are promised a better life if they only give up their striving to establish democracy. Even in the West the free institutions of democracy are belittled and insulted.

The fires under the cauldron of class hatred and ideological intolerance are burning fiercely. Our democratic freedom is the target. Yes, our political democracy can be endan-

9

gered in this interdependent world by outside forces. The West accepted the challenge of the totalitarian Communist forces and now the Communist world is sorely pressed. There is not enough room on this small globe for two such diametrically opposed ideologies as totalitarianism and democracy. The Communist dictators tremble for their regime and for their own life under the potential menace of the terrific military might of the West and under the possible attraction of its free democratic institutions. In this situation, which has been developed by their initial aggressiveness, they can not but press their attack on the Western democracies. Neither can the Western camp relax without the risk of being taken in. The smallest opening might prove large enough for a cunning and resolute enemy to break through the defences or to smuggle in a Trojan horse to invade the West from inside.

The totalitarian forces are seeking to destroy our freedom because we are doing everything short of war to lay open their false promises and expose the personal crimes of their leaders. The West is determined to extinguish all forces menacing democracy and freedom. The cold war of ideologies is a deadly serious matter.

Yes, the world cannot remain long half-free and half-slave. In the long run every nation will be free or it will be slave. Freedom is as internationally interdependent as is peace and prosperity. In an ideologically interdependent world no nation can any more have freedom and political democracy alone. This world, and all nations in it, are interdependent not only in the economic sense and as far as security is concerned. All nations are also interdependent in the political sense as ideologies are pressed with great force before the broadest masses of all continents.

Ever since the First World War we have been talking about the indivisibility of peace, which is the consequence of the interdependent security of the nations. Peace is indivisible indeed. Two new expressions will be heard more and more in the coming years: the indivisibility of prosperity and the indivisibility of freedom. The prosperity of the world became also indivisible as the consequence of economic interdependence. The freedom of all nations can also be said to be indivisible because of the ideological interdependence of the nations of the world. No one nation alone can have peace. No nation alone can have prosperity any more. No nation can have freedom alone.

We, the people of the world, will live in peace, or we will go down together in destruction. We, the people of the world, will have to build a prosperous world together, or all will share in the destitution of the present misery-ridden part of the globe. We, the people of the world will live in freedom together, or we all will deliver ourselves into slavery. We either create a happy and a good world together or expose ourselves to the dangers of universal destruction, poverty, and slavery.

Warning signals are not missing to alert us to the wrongs of the world. World war, world depression, and world revolution are ominous words enough. They counsel us to undertake the necessary steps on the international level to forestall a world cataclysm. We already have had two world wars; they were terrible enough. They warned us about the deadly seriousness of the international interdependence of security. Have they cautioned us enough about the little time left to organize the world for peace?

We already have had a world depression and it was serious enough. It took us a long time to recover. We in America might try to build into our economy so-called depression-absorbing and safety devices. No completely depression-proof national economy can exist in this economically interdependent world of ours. World depression, in spite of what-ever the nation-states try to do to prevent it, remains a distinct possibility which might bring us, the people of the world, down again together.

Nor can we take too lightly the menace of world revolution. We came pretty close to it after the two world wars. Today this warning signal is looming on the horizon larger than ever before, because it is backed up by one of the greatest physical forces ever built by man. Not only is world communism as an ideology behind the plan of world revolution. It is the physical power of the Soviet Union which makes the danger of a world revolution very real.

International interdependence is, then, a fact. After having considered all its aspects, we have to add that it is the most important fact of our day. It is a fact which should be soberly considered by all of us. It is a fact that imposes, or should impose, very definite responsibilities on each of us lest tragedy overtake the world. Let us act, before the next blow hits us hard. Hit us hard it will, if we do not prevent the disaster by meaningful, intelligent, and resolute action.

What are then the requirements? What are the directives in today's menacing situation consequent upon the world's becoming an interdependent unit?

We have an interdependent world, but man does not seem to be aware of all its implications. We do not have a world community of feeling. Nor do we have authority to take care of all the interlinking, common problems which multiply with the onrush of time and with the intensification of our technical and industrial civilization.

Common problems, problems which cross the national boundaries and transcend the capability and the qualifications of the individual nation-states to solve them, should be solved by an international forum made able and equipped to do so.

We still live in a period when the nation-state is still the sovereign unit of man's political co-operation. However, the nation-state can not solve problems which transcend the national territory and demand international solution. The nation-state is no longer in a position to take care of the security and the well-being of its individual citizens because their security and well-being depend ultimately on forces beyond the control of the nation-state.

Is the nation-state, or those who lead it, conscious of its shortcomings brought about by the gradually developed international interdependence of the world? Is the nation-state willing to adjust to the facts? Is it willing to consider the most important change in our time: the rise of an interdependent world community? (This world community might not exist legally but it certainly exists factually). Are the eighty or ninety nation-states of the world doing anything really meaningful to cede some of their attributes of statehood to an international organization? Are they doing anything purposeful to delegate some of their sovereignty to an all-embracing world organization? Is it clear to them that the interests of their individual citizens require and urgently demand such action?

Nobody can see into the future. The past records would indicate that through trials and errors, causing terrible sufferings and involving sacrifices of great values, man falteringly but always surely has found the needed solutions to the new problems of an ever-changing world. History seems to testify to the fact that man, despite his failures and sins, despite wounds and defeat, despite much erring and often despite loss of the true direction itself, more driven than driving, finally does shape up to the requirements of his times and is able to cope with his new situations. God is with him.

Man is now standing in the gateway of a new era, that of human unification. (Or shall we call it reunification?) The new era will come. But will man go right through the open gateway? Or will he keep knocking his head foolishly against the wall, as historic facts indicate that he usually does? Will the new era come through terrible trials and bloody errors? Will the world be shaken by world wars, world depressions, and world revolutions? Will many millions have to lay down their lives unnecessarily? Will the new world have to be built on the ruins of the old? Or will man this time have enough sense to modernize and reinforce the old structure in time? Will he adjust his ways to the requirements of an interdependent world, in order to forestall the impending tragedy? Above all, will man listen to the voice of Christianity which is ready to tender wise counsel for the solution of this most important and difficult problem?

What stands then in the way of the sensible solution of the common problems of all peoples? What stands in the way of building a purposeful international organization equipped with all the necessary means to accomplish its purpose: to prevent war, to relieve the misery-ridden masses of the world and to bring about world democracy?

Nobody can deny the fact that this world is interdependent. Nobody can deny that all the nations depend on each other. Nobody can deny that there could be no peace, no prosperity, and no freedom for any individual nation alone.

But, are we willing to draw all the consequences from the interdependence of the nations? Are the nation-states willing to participate in the building of an international organization equipped with all necessary means to guarantee international peace, to bring general prosperity, and to establish freedom for all?

Then what should be the attributes of an international organization able to fulfill its mission to bring peace, prosperity, and freedom for all?

Such a world organization, first, should have power. Yes, physical power, sheer force. Whatever high or spiritual aspiration man might have, he is not only a spiritual being, he is also materialistic. Besides needing spiritual inspiration, man also needs coercion. Wherever people organize for political action, authority backed up with physical and enforcing power has to be provided for. International organization can not be an exception to this rule.

A purposeful international organization, to be set up by the nations in the interest of their own citizens, also needs *direct* access to the individual human beings. An organization in itself, separate from its individual human members, is lifeless. It cannot function. It cannot fulfil its mission in the abstract; it can function only through its human members. An organization functions through the agency of its individual human members. No political organization can expect to accomplish anything unless it can address itself *directly* to human individuals in order to make them do something or to make them refrain from doing something. If a political organization is unable to reach individual human beings *directly,* its chances to succeed in its mission are nil. If a union of nations has to ask the permission of the component states before acting through individual persons, which is the only possible way to act, then it is paralyzed from its very inception.

The third postulate of the international organization which is needed for solving the problems of peace, prosperity, and freedom, is no less important. According to the principle of democracy, the people make the government and they also defeat and remake it. In a democracy all decisions ultimately are up to the people. The government is only the agency of the people to carry out their mandate. As a corollary to these rights the people carry all the responsibility in a democratically governed political community. The fate of a democratic state reposes in the hands of its citizens. In order to be able to live up to this responsibility the individuals should have the feeling that the political community of which they are members belongs to them. They must identify their interests with the interests of the community. They must do more. They must be willing to sacrifice their own interests to those of their community. They should be willing to pay taxes, for instance, until it hurts them. They should be willing to offer the supreme sacrifice which a community demands: to give their own lives and the lives of their beloved ones in order that the community may live.

To be a loyal member of a political community requires many sacrifices. Appeal to reason is not enough to make man willing to sacrifice his personal interest to that of the community. It is true, man is a rational being. But he is also an emotional being. Last, but not least, he is selfish and egotistic. Man could not overcome his self-interest, his inclination not to part with his earthly possessions, his instinct of survival— if only his intelligence would urge him to do so. Emotional forces have to be brought into play. The nation-state is a "going" concern because, among other things, its citizens are attached to it by strong ties of emotional forces. No democratic political organization could survive without the sentimental attachment of its human members. It could not survive without the love of the members toward their country.

The international organization which is needed for solving the problems of peace, prosperity, and freedom for all nations can be built only upon democratic principles. Therefore it also needs the sentimental attachment of the individual human beings who unite within its fold for the protection of their interests. It is true that men should understand the necessity of establishing such an organization and should have the will to go ahead and do the job. Intelligence and will are necessary to succeed. But something more is needed. Men need emotional inspiration for the work to establish an international organization commensurate with the need. After such an international organization is established, it will have to claim for its very survival not only the obedience but also the love of the people of the world.

We enumerated the three most important attributes necessary to enable the needed international organization to carry out its mission. Let us see, now, whether the three requirements of a purposeful international organization would be forthcoming under the present circumstances. Without hesitation one can state that the attributes required for a successful international organization are monopolized, at least for the time being, by the sovereign nation-states. Point by point we will look at the present situation as far as the three requirements are concerned.

First, the nation-states divide among themselves all existing physical force. All coercive power existing on the face of the earth is under the control of the sovereign states. All the weapons are controlled by the eighty or ninety (the number is constantly changing with the establishment of new countries) nation-states. Legally nobody can own any weapon anywhere in the world except with the permission of a nation-state. Weapons of greater size or force are owned by the states alone (warships, airplanes, tanks, self-propelled missiles, cannons, etc.). Smaller arms, such as guns and revolvers, are also under the jurisdictional control of the nation-states. No physical force is left for any international organization.

Second, nation-states have direct access to their nationals. The nation-state alone holds the full control of its citizens. The nation-state can reach them day and night and can command whatever it wants them to do. Only the state can command human beings to refrain from doing something; for instance, from paying any attention to the recommendations of the United Nations.

All living human beings reside on the territory of one or another state. They all are subject to the unlimited jurisdiction of the states where they reside. All the territory of the globe is divided among nation-states. No land-territory remains unclaimed. Human beings have no other choice; they must live in the territory of some state. Nor is any human individual left without nationality, that is, without a legal tie to a state. With the exception of a negligible number of stateless persons, everybody is a citizen of some state. But

16

stateless or not, citizens or not, as has been said before, human beings live on some state's territory because all territory is divided up among states. Everybody is, therefore, subject to a state, which claims sovereignty over the territory of his residence.

No human being is left for the international organization to reach directly. An international organization has no direct access to any individual person. Not a single person in the world can put himself at the disposal of an international organization without the permission of his country. The international organization cannot accomplish anything unless the sovereign state under whose jurisdiction the individual resides will authorize such action as the international organization wants the particular individual to perform. International organizations will be check-mated until they are given direct access to individual human beings.

The third attribute of a purposeful international organization is also withheld by the nation-state. Individual states insist that their citizens owe to them and only to them complete, undivided, and unhesitating loyalty and love. All the loyalty an individual human being can muster has to be reserved for the state. All his love is supposed to belong exclusively to his state. The individual's allegiance to his nation is freely given, and is taken for granted by the state. The motivating force behind this emotional attachment is nationalism, a formidable power of historic importance. The true measure of nationalism is demonstrated by the willingness of man to lay down his life for his country. It is because of nationalism that man is first of all a Frenchman, a German, a Hungarian, or an American. Only in the second place does man dare to be or to think and act in terms of a human being. Man as a political being does not dare to think and act as a member of the human race. Nationalism is the reason why the primary loyalty of modern man is given to his nation and his country. The loyalty to one's own nation-state completely overshadows the relations of modern man to any other human group. No group loyalty can even approximate the intensity of nationalism in the heart of today's man. (Beyond all sentimental cause the real explanation for this phenomenon is the knowledge that only the state can enforce the loyalty which it commands.) Even the loyalty to one's church and religion is receding before the impelling force of nationalism. Should allegiance to one's nation conflict with loyalty to one's church, without any question religious loyalty would have to give place. Church relations are relegated in our modern life to secondary rank. They are subordinated to what is considered as state interest.

The nation-state does not (and if it desired to keep its predominant position in modern life it can not) stand for divided loyalty. The nation-state not only jealously watches the individual so that he should not look beyond the nation's boundary; it also forbids him to divide his loyalty between the state and other groups within the nation.

With this all-absorbing force of nationalism, how could an international organization hope to raise in the heart of the individual any feeling of emotional attachment? How could a nationalist feel love for an international organization? Can the United Nations be loved while man's heart is bursting with love for his own nation?

The conclusion is clear: all the factors which make a political community potent are withheld by the nation-state. Only the state has physical power. Only the state has direct access to individual human beings. Only the state is permitted to awaken love in the hearts of men. To put it simply, the nation-state is the sovereign and not the international organization. Yet unless the international organization becomes sovereign it will remain unable to carry out the great mission which until such time will have to wait to be accomplished. With the nation-state the undisputed master, the assurance of undisturbed peace, secured prosperity, and guaranteed freedom will have to wait.

Meanwhile the nation-state is not willing to abdicate its sovereignty. It is not even considering to limit it. It is problematical whether it even would be willing to delegate part of its sovereignty to international organizations.

The nation-state is self-motivated, self-centered, and self-perpetuating. It is self-motivated because it acts in terms of its own aims and not necessarily in the interests of the individual human beings who make up the state. The nation-state is self-centered because it looks at the problems of world organization from the point of view of its own existence and not from that of the interests of the individual citizens. The nation-state is self-perpetuating because it is not willing to abdicate its sovereignty and step down from its exalted position of uncontested political predominance and omnipotence. It is not ready to transform itself to a more modest instrument of man's political activity. It is not willing to recognize its own inability to assure the security and the well-being of its individual citizens. To state it briefly, it does not want to cease to exist as the supreme territorial sovereign with ultimate power of life and death over human beings.

Here is the root of the troubles of our present time. Here we come to the core of the prevailing impasse of international relations. Man's peace, man's well-being, and man's freedom cannot be assured, simply because the largest and the only sovereign political organization, i.e. the nation-state, is no longer in a position to guarantee those values for the individual. It is beyond its ability to do so. Yet, it is unwilling to let the individual human beings form a larger unit with sovereign power, which would then be in the position to attend to the satisfaction of those individual needs with which the nation-state can not cope. Only the nation-states could make the international organization sovereign, because only they possess sovereignty. The growing number of problems of international scope remain unsolved because the nation-state cannot solve them and is reluctant to create an international organization equipped to cope with them. Man's universal problems, unsolved as they remain or only partly and insufficiently solved as they are, cause troubles. They are bound to cause more trouble as international interdependence intensifies. Dangers of formidable magnitude are menacing mankind.

2. BOLSHEVIK-COMMUNISM

We now have described international interdependence, a most important fact of today's international relations. We observed that man has not yet drawn the necessary consequences from this fact because the sovereign nation-state is hindering the creation of a meaningful political community of world-wide scope.

We live in a period of transition when man is struggling to end the impasse in the development of international relations. This impasse consists in the fact that man has become stalled at the last stage of territorial integration, the stage of nation-states. The problem calls for a solution consistent with the past: for the creation of a larger territorial unit, large enough to cope with all the problems created by the fact of international interdependence.

This is the problem. It is not hard to understand. Modern man's predicament in our twentieth century can be understood readily. It is not only the student and the scholar who are concerned with the most urgent and most important problem of the human race, namely, the survival of our civilization. The common man is also sensing the impending catastrophe, which will be on us if we do not prevent it by intelligent and responsible action.

Furthermore, the fact that the common man understands the situation and senses the cause of mankind's predicament raises a corollary problem: Bolshevik-communism. Marxism holds out false promises to the common man. It promises an end to all the troubles of the world. It pictures a better future for man. In essence its promise is two-fold. First, it pledges international peace in a communist world to be established on the ruins of the "capitalist dominated" present state system after the heralded victory of the proletarian world revolution. Secondly, Bolshevik-communism promises an end to the poverty of the hundreds of millions of wage earners by the socialization of the means of production and distribution.

Bolshevik-communism is not the ailment; rather, it is the symptom of the sickness. The world was sick before its spectacular rise; war was a permanent plague and poverty an ever-present affliction. Bolshevism, instead of being the malaise itself, is simply evidence that something is wrong with the world. Should we even succeed in erasing the Soviet Union from the face of the earth, the wrong which caused the sickness would still remain. By clearing up the symptom we do not cure the patient. The only way to get rid of the malady is to eliminate the cause.

The very things which today are sickening the world also explain the rise of Bolshevik-communism. Communism is thriving on the unsolved problems of war and human misery. Men all over the world are craving for peace; they are disgusted with war. Men all over the world are hungering for economic security. They do not take poverty for granted any more. They are more than willing to listen to the logical-sounding theories that hold out salvation from the disasters of war and the misery of poverty. Bolshevik-communism is spreading all over the world because it promises an end to wars in a world where the danger of war is always around the corner. Communism is tempting many hundred millions because, in spite of all the technical progress and "know-how" of the West, by far the greater part of the world's population is still living under the most miserable economic conditions. Such false prophets of communism as Marx, Engels, and Lenin claim that only they have a solution for the problems of war and poverty.

Man is tired of war. The misery-ridden masses know that there is a way to a better life for them. Communism has above all an appeal to the hundreds of millions of hungry, misery-ridden Asians and Africans. It also has an appeal to the dissatisfied masses of war-weary Europe. It is also a great potential menace in Latin-America, where millions are living in ignorance and misery.

The United States dares ignore the danger of Communism only at its own risk. In case of a depression the Communists would find willing support among its people. Most of the Communist sympathizers and some of the traitors actually did mature into adult life during the depression-hit early

Thirties. In an economically interdependent world the economy of this country is not depression-proof. The prosperity of this nation is not only dependent on what the American people do. A depression can be brought on us from outside sources. This is the great hope of the Communist leaders. They would more than welcome a depression in the United States. Already they have bent all their efforts to bring about a depression in our country. They would not shy away from cutting off this nation from its foreign raw material sources and from its foreign markets. Their greatest ambition is to isolate economically the United States from the rest of the world. Then in a depression-stricken country the soil would be prepared for subversion and infiltration.

The communist leaders, indeed, well understand the aspiration of the masses. This is vividly illustrated by the picture of the United States they paint before the people of the world. They depict the United States as the headquarters of war-mongering and the worst kind of militarism. They also claim this country to be the fountainhead of capitalism, the evil which is supposedly responsible for the backwardness and poverty of the Asian, African, South American, and European masses. They want the war-weary and misery-ridden people to turn against America which they describe as being the personification of war-mongering militarism and predatory materialism.

If the West wants to get rid of Bolshevik-communism, the best it can do is to eliminate the causes of the sickness in our modern world. Prominent factors are the permanent danger of war, the human misery prevailing in the greater part of the world, and above all the fact that man does not seem to direct his steps toward the creation of an institutionalized world community for abolishing war and poverty. If the West desires to be victor in the cold war, it has to try to organize the people of the world in a universal effort for the institutionalized elimination of the plague of war and the same of poverty. We know that Communism thrives on wars and poverty; hence with their disappearance it is bound to wither away.

In the meanwhile Bolshevik-communism rather hampers man in his search for a life of peace, prosperity, and freedom.

It considerably complicates an already complex and troubled situation. It confuses people and it fools them. It does not mean what it says. It is a road-block on the way towards a meaningful international organization.

As far as Communism's relation to freedom is concerned, not too many people can be fooled. Freedom is the Achillean heel of Bolshevik-communism. Although peace and the promise of material well-being are on their lips, Communist propagandists are much less talkative about the freedom of the individual and political freedom. A good look at the Communist-dominated countries explains their concentration on peace and well-being in their propaganda and their reluctance to talk about freedom. In Communist countries no individual or political freedom exists. In politics the Soviet Union openly accepted the dictatorship of the proletariat which in practice means the dictatorship of the Communist party, that is, of the party leader or leaders. The Communist regime is totalitarian. It discarded democracy. Man does not have much achievement behind him, but thanks to Christianity Western man has succeeded in establishing the best political form of human co-existence and co-operation: political democracy. How could one call an idea progressive if the first thing its advocates do wherever they take over is to bring down political democracy and with it human freedom?

It is not surprising, then, that the leaders of world Communism, after eliminating political democracy (the great achievement of Western man), sold down the river even those progressive-sounding ideas which originally they claimed to uphold. Peace is on their lips only for propaganda purposes. If ever they were sure to win by aggression against incomparably weaker nations, they did not shy away from attacking them. (It should be enough to recall their infamous winter aggression against little Finland in 1939-1940). The Communist leaders are doing nothing to eliminate the causes of war. Why should they? They thrive on war. The First World War started them on their career. History shows that defeated nations are the first to be tempted to accept Bolshevik-communism. The Soviet Union grew to its present power as the result of the Second World War.

Its leaders hint that they expect to take over the world after the Third World War. War seems to work for them. Instead of eliminating the causes of war they add new ones to the list. Ideological war and class war are their invention.

With the case of Communist Yugoslavia fresh in our mind, we very much doubt that peace would prevail in a Communist world among Communist states. After breaking with Yugoslavia the Soviet Union did everything in its power to destroy that country and was busily preparing to mount an attack on Tito's land. Had it not been for American help to Yugoslavia, it is highly probable that the Russian army or the armies of the "loyal" satellites would have brutally invaded their fellow-Communist country. The world then would have witnessed a war between Communist countries whose most effective slogan to the war-weary people of the globe is the promise of peace.

Nor is it surprising that, wherever they take over, they forget about their promise of a better, more abundant life for the masses. The Communist regimes enchain individual human beings and sacrifice their well-being on the altar of the party interest and exploit individuals for the sake of the Communist state. The Communist leaders do not sincerely desire to assist the poverty-stricken peoples and nations. The poorer a country is, the more chance the party faithful have to take it over. Why should the local Communist party work for the well-being of the people, if prosperity would put its leaders out of business? On the other hand, once in power, by totalitarian state-craft the Communists can disregard the wishes and aspirations of their own people. Because they are not responsible to their people, they do not have to consider the people's wishes concerning the improvement of their well-being.

In spite of all the false pretenses, Bolshevik-communism fools many. Numerous progressive-minded men and women of unimpeachable morals and ideals, who would have fought for international democracy and for a more humane world, were lured by false pretensions of progressiveness to the Communist camp. Only a few such as Arthur Koestler, André Gide, and Whittaker Chambers found their way back. The masses were duped by false promises and high-sounding but empty slogans.

Bolshevism deters men from the road leading to international co-operation inspired by Christianity. In the present cold war situation the important issue is side-tracked. People are confused. Progressive elements are divided. Time is lost. Unimportant ideological issues are infused into man's mind. They are poisoning the atmosphere. Nations are divided internally along class lines. Class struggle is emphasized. Hatred is germinated when man is badly in need of love. War, instead of being abolished, is looming larger and larger on the horizon.

As far as the attitude of Communist leaders towards international organizations is concerned, it is very revealing to know how reluctant the USSR was to help establish a strong international organization. The Communist leaders were not at all enthusiastic about the plan to build the United Nations. They were pressing for concessions, trying to make the planned organization as weak and as powerless as possible. It is good also to recall how keenly they fought all propositions aimed at the limitation of the sovereignty of the member states. They felt so strongly about this that several times they let it be known that they would not join the planned organization unless their opposition to a stronger United Nations was heeded. More than one sick and gravely afflicted American statesman such as President Roosevelt and his personal advisor, Harry Hopkins, had to make long trips and undertake special missions to the Soviet Union to entice dictator Stalin to make minor concessions, and this often at a price out of proportion with Stalin's concessions. At the San Francisco conference the Communist delegates were the most uncompromising advocates of the predominance of the great powers within the United Nations. The U.S.S.R. was responsible more than any other great power for obtaining special privileges for the permanent members of the Security Council, and in general guaranteeing favored standing to the Great Powers within the United Nations. Nor did the Soviet Union change its obstruction against a stronger and more effective international organization after the United Nations began to function. Many promising international actions aimed at the general welfare of the world were nipped in the bud by Russia's wholesale use of the veto. Nor should we ignore the fact that the Soviet Union repeatedly stalled on the functioning of the specialized agencies of the United Nations.

The Soviet Union is hampering in every way the working of international organizations meant to relieve the pains of the world. The Communist powers do not stand for consolidation inasmuch as they thrive on disorders and actually profit from troubles. The Soviet Union is not for democratic world co-operation and democratic internationalism. It has its own pattern of world government. Its ultimate aim calls for the realization of the Communist world-state. However, even in the Communist sphere the idea of co-operation, for the Russian, spells domination by the USSR. Among the Communist states Russia has to be always right. (This does not refer to the special relation between Russia and China).

Internationalism, indeed, is on the lips of the Russian Communist leaders in order to make it easier for them to penetrate foreign countries. But at home they are real super-patriots who claim all discoveries and all achievements of the past or the present for Russia. Nor are they, in spite of all their preaching about racial equality and minority rights, tolerant toward their own racial and other minorities.

False prophets never can help a good cause. False doctrines are not condusive to right solutions. The cause of world peace, world prosperity, and world freedom is rather hampered than helped by the international Communist conspiracy. The global split brought about by Bolshevik-communism only complicates matters. Its materialistic doctrine, its ruthless totalitarian practices do not speak for progress. They stand in diametrical opposition to the moral values upheld by Christian international democracy.

We are aware of the changes which have occurred in the Soviet Union since the death of Stalin. Some of our statements are based more on what happened while Stalin ruled than on events during the few years which have elapsed since the so-called collective leadership took over. However, up to now the essence of the Communist rule has not changed. The dictatorship remains. The desire to take-over the world is not given up. Military preparation is pressed. Economic competition is stepped up. The new dictators are shrewd enough to talk with the voice of the sirens but they still serve Mars.

The situation might change. Real concessions might follow the softer talk, but for the time being nothing indicates any fundamental change in Soviet policy.

3. DESPIRITUALIZED THOUGHT AND LIFE

The difficulties, as we saw them, on the road towards meaningful international organization are considerable. Both ultra-nationalistic and Bolshevik-communistic forces are in the way. Most of the people are aware of the tremendous difficulties. Probably most of them do not even consider realistic the plans to build a political world community. They label as dreamers those who have faith in man's ability to solve the problems of war and poverty. They do not believe that man can overcome the impediments of nationalism. Confronted with tremendous hindrances, man becomes defeatist or "realist." The ability to see the opening of a new horizon is not given to all. The average modern man does not have enough faith. To overcome deep-rooted conventions and the formidable hindrance of inertia which has been accumulated through many centuries requires faith.

No less difficulty is involved in fighting the temptation of Bolshevik-communism and its organized forces. It is true that Communism thrives on the fact that Western man was unable to solve the problems of war and poverty. But it is likewise true that the quick rise of world Communism can be explained also by the fact that the world in which it arose had lost its spiritual foundation and its faith in transcendent values. Communism found a response in the hearts of millions not only because it promised peace and well-being to the war-weary and the hungry, but also because Western man had lost his faith in God. Communism for many is a substitute for real religion, which under the still prevailing materialistic philosophy of the West has gradually been relegated to secondary rank in the thought and life of modern man.

Western man is facing the tremendous task of organizing the world for peace and prosperity. He is challenged at the same time by Bolshevik-communism. To cope with these formidable problems man has to have faith. Man must have ideals. He has to be convinced that he is on the right road. He has to believe that he will be able to reach the high goal of universal human co-operation, and with it a more abundant life. This conviction will be his only if he has faith, especially the confidence in his ability to live up to his great assignment. He can have faith in himself only through faith in his God.

We want to emphasize again that in his attempt to overcome retrograde forces of ultra-nationalism man faces formidable hindrances, which he can eliminate only if he lifts himself to the heights of purest spiritual considerations. Man will be able to cope with the requirements of an inter-dependent world only if he will be inspired by spiritual aspirations. But spiritual aspirations will come to him only by faith, not in himself alone, but faith in his God. Man's faith in himself comes through faith in his Creator.

We repeat here again, because it cannot be said often enough, that in order to take up the challenge of Bolshevik-communism man has to be interested in something more than in his material well-being. He has to be able to raise his sights above the material problems of the world if he wants to win over the Communist temptation. It is true that the Communists themselves are above all interested in the material side of life and their teaching is based on the so-called doctrine of dialectical materialism. However, it should be recognized that notwithstanding all their professed theo retical materialism, they are also perfectly aware of the fact that "man does not live by bread alone." The Communist party requires (as is generally known) complete subordina-tion from the party member to the Communist movement. It demands self-sacrifice from its devotees. It commands them to sacrifice egoistic considerations on the altar of the party. The Communists teach their partisans to live and, if need be, to die for their party. The Communist countries require renunciation of self-interest from the present generation by promising a better life to the coming generations. While the Communist leaders of the Soviet Union have deviated far from their ideals in their private lives, nonetheless they seem to hold countless millions under the spell of their ideology. This influence comes only partly from the loudly proclaimed identification of the Communist party with the material interests of the working classes. The successes of the party can also be explained by the fact that it inspires its partisans with the feeling of being part of a higher mission which they say is bound to win as it is based on principles of justice and truth. The Communist propaganda clearly vindicates higher values to its own movement when it brands the West as "profit hungry," "money obsessed," and when it refers to the Western leaders as the "tools of world-capitalism" and "exploiters of the workers."

The greatest menace of Communism consists in the fact that it provides its partisans with ideals to believe in, ideals to have faith in and to fight for. Though these ideals are based on false foundations, they provide inspiration for action. They are false, but if the Communist devotee believes strongly in them, he will fight with all the fury a fanatic can work up in himself. In his fight with Communism, Western man has to contend with the fact that the challenger is not devoid of spiritual weapons. Even if these weapons are fraudulent, they are nonetheless formidable. Western man has not much possibility of overcoming the temptation of the false doctrine unless he is armed with genuine spiritual weapons as well as with material ones. The West will not be able to win over the danger of Communism unless it is inspired by spiritual values.

It is the greatest imaginable tragedy of modern man that, along with his material progress, he despiritualized his thought and life. It is a great tragedy, indeed, that while man became able to control the forces of nature and succeeded in learning how to use them to improve his material standards, he forgot about God who had endowed him with intelligence to invent and apply his inventions for material progress. The age of reason, the age of industry, became also the age of skepticism and the age of doubt as far as the transcending values were concerned. Reason, which should go hand in hand with faith, became autonomous. The great inventions of our age which could help in the establishment of permanent peace and the bringing about of world prosperity and freedom for all could also cause man to plunge into the abyss of self-destructive war. Thus they could end the prosperity which some very privileged nations now enjoy. They could be used to exterminate political democracy in the few Western countries which had the special opportunity to establish free institutions. It is a tragedy that although man has in his hands the technical means to create a peaceful, abundant, and free world, he faces the danger that he will destroy civilization with these same means and with his own hands.

Man can be justly proud of the material achievements of the modern age. However, he is not able to control the forces which he has unchained. While the forces of nature are at his disposal, it is questionable whether he will use these forces for good or for evil. He has the choice of bringing about a better world or of plunging into war and thereby destroying civilization. He has the choice of using the new energies of terrific force to create a good life or to destroy himself. While his intelligence helps him to see these terrible alternatives, he is himself not sure what he will do: choose the good road or go the fatal way. He can consult his intellect, but more than intelligence is required. The respect for spiritual values alone can hold him back from choosing the evil road. Although man, a reasonable being, knows that he faces destruction at his own hands, should a Third World War come, he is unable to escape the fate he fears unless spiritual considerations make him drop the weapons he has devised to be used in such a suicidal war. The control of the enchained forces of potential destruction can be assured only when spiritual values are given the same importance as material values.

However, in the mind of modern man material considerations prevail. How did this situation develop? How did it come that man dropped his spiritual armor? How could it happen that man despiritualized his thought and his life? In order to answer these questions, we have to take a quick look at the history of man's thought, especially at the development of modern thought.

All the great civilizations were based on spiritual foundations. Their spiritual values were in turn supported by their religious beliefs. Material achievements are safe only when they are based on spiritual values. A civilization is shaken to its very foundation if it robs itself of its spiritual heritage and if it condones the worship of material idols. Great things can be achieved only under the inspiration of great ideals.

All through history we can observe the closest relationship between earthly human considerations and high spiritual aspirations. If the two are in balance man progresses, achieves great things, and his soul is at ease. In such harmonious epochs man's feet are firmly planted on the ground, but he lifts his vision to the skies. Civilizations have grown under religious inspiration.

We do not imply that all religions are right. We do not even suggest that man cannot live without religion. What we believe is that man cannot live in peace without being supported by a strong belief in spiritual values. All ancient civilizations grew on spiritual inspirations. Most of them had religious foundations. It is almost impossible to separate the community life of the ancient Egyptians and the contemporaneous Mesopotanian people from their religion. This is also true of Persia and the rest of the empires of the ancient Near and Middle East. Arab caliphates fused the political and religious leadership in the person of the ruling caliph. The civilization of the Indian subcontinent was and partly still is based on Hinduism. While Confucianism is not a religion but rather a way of life or a philosophy, it is based on lofty spiritual aspirations of man.

These historic instances do not prove that the ancient people had a good life and that justice prevailed among them. What they indicate is that while the accepted moral standards, based on religion or spiritual values, were respected in the ancient lands, the people there lived in social harmony and domestic peace.

Spiritual considerations held the same role also among the Greeks and the Romans. Their gods were an integral part of their daily lives and religious ideas permeated the atmosphere in which they lived. The great Greek philosophers such as Socrates, Plato, and Aristotle stood for the highest spiritual values. Their interests were focused on the problems of truth, justice, and the good life. Their moral philosophy is the crowning achievement of the Hellenic age. It is not an accident that the greatness of Athens was contemporaneous with the golden age of the Athenean philosophy. The importance of philosophy in supplying moral and spiritual values was best proven by the part that Stoic philosophy played in the preparation of the world for the acceptance of Christianity.

During the Middle Ages the totality of political, social, cultural, and economic life was deeply influenced by Christianity as understood and more often misunderstood by the medieval man. Despite all the darkness of the Middle Ages, medieval Christian Europe was more a spiritual than a political unit. Religion dominated the scene. Some of the great Christian philosophers, such as Thomas Aquinas, not only left a deep imprint on their times; actually their spiritual influence is very keenly felt in our own days.

With the coming of the modern age a despiritualizing process set in. The gradual despiritualization of the life and thought of modern man led him right to his present predicament, wherein he finds himself unable either to cope with the problems of war and misery, or to fight against the temptation of false solutions and false hopes.

The new philosophical trend, which ultimately led man to the despiritualization of his thought and life, began with the great successes scored by the researchers in the field of physics and astronomy. Through the achievements of Kepler, Copernicus, Galileo, and Newton many new laws of physics were laid down, transforming man's conception of the universe. Philosophers and social scientists were greatly impressed by the successes in natural science and were more and more tempted to imitate the methods that were used by natural scientists.

At the beginning of the process of secularization the aim seemed to have been only to liberate man's reason from the darkness of superstition and ignorance. The fight started in the sixteenth century for the recognition of the autonomy of the human reason and for the acceptance of the supreme worth of every individual. The prevailing philosophical thought of the seventeenth century even argued for the reasonableness of Christianity, as we see in John Locke. Revelation did not seem to contradict reason for these philosophers. The trend, however, emphasized reason more

33

and more and de-emphasized faith. So it happened that philosophy soon ceased to try to reconcile Christianity with science and eliminated Christian revelation altogether as being contradictory to reason. This change still let God stand for a while, but only as a presupposition to prove the existence of man's reason, as Descartes claimed. The creation of man with his reason was conveniently explained by the deists as God's work. The logical process of despiritualization did not stop long at this stage. During the "enlightened" eighteenth century God himself was frontally attacked and eliminated without much ceremony. Substitutes were not hard to find.

Some philosophers of the enlightened brand, like Condorcet, kept on worshipping reason and went so far on this road that they became unreasonable enough to write even about man's conquest over death. Some worshiped progress and others glorified nature. There were philosophers who, though agreeing with the rest as far as God's demise was concerned, at the same time attacked the worship of reason. Thus Rousseau advised man to follow the urge of his own natural instinct as the best way to salvation. By the end of the eighteenth century David Hume began to doubt the truth of his own theory.

The rise of the nineteenth century saw the coming of the utilitarian philosophers such as Bentham and John Stuart Mill. Inspired by their theories, liberal politicians were able to take over or exercise influence on their respective governments in such countries as Great Britain, France, and Italy. The worship of the autonomous individual and the belief in the essential goodness of man acted as a solvent of all former community ties and set free the individual human being to act as his own personal utilitarian interest would dictate. Some of the utilitarian liberals, including Adam Smith, could even reconcile this philosophy with the mystic vision of an "unseen hand" as directing the egoistic action of the individual for the final good of all mankind.

During the nineteenth century the students of natural sciences continued to score spectacular successes in explaining natural phenomena and in subjecting nature's forces to the use of man. Philosophers fell more and more under the spell of natural science. Those who proudly called themselves positivists undertook the arduous task of re-shaping social sciences on the pattern and according to the rules of natural sciences, but this was an impossible job. Led by Auguste Comte and Herbert Spencer, they were striving for a unified view of both natural and human phenomena. Comte himself preached the need for a new religion to take the place of Christianity and advocated the worship of humanity instead of God. Their new science, sociology, aimed to bring a bright future with per-fect order and social harmony.

All these various schools of thought in liberal philosophy, though divergent and sometimes even conflicting, mirrored the prevailing optimistic mood of the nineteenth century. Their advocates were convinced that the human race faced a brilliant future and that progress had practically no limits. With the positivist the last shred of human modesty and moderation disappeared from the philosophy of Western man.

The philosophers in the school of idealism (so-called) were no more moderate or responsible in their thought. Hegel, for instance, believed so intensely in his idea of historic dialecticism that he was inclined to equate God with history. He became so enamored with his historic conception of the modern state that he considered it to be the "march of God in history."

It is not at all surprising that in this jungle of irresponsible ideas and arbitrary philosophical concepts—namely, with the interest of the masterless man reigning supreme, with human society atomized, with man robbed of his interest in the problem of eternity—Marxist socialism was eagerly accepted by the lower classes. Classical liberal philosophy of the nineteenth century completely disregarded the in-terests of the industrial labor class. It is not surprising that a soulless society, one that indulged in material pleasures, that was deprived of spiritual consideration, itself faithless and godless, could not offer much resistance to the rising tide of totalitarian forces. The nineteenth century middle-class states of Western Europe, with the

35

possible exception of Great Britain, lacked the necessary spiritual values and moral stamina to take up the challenge of Marxism.

Essentially Marxism posed as the defender of the human community against the uncontrolled predatory instincts of the individual. It presented a well-reasoned plan for a better life as against the hazards involved in the liberal conception of letting nature's forces take their course whatever the cost for the unprotected lower classes. Marxism, with its deterministic self-assurance based on the certainty of the historic dialectical process, had a special appeal to the misery-ridden masses. Its success can also be explained if one considers it a quasi-religion to fill in the gap opened in man's soul by the despiritualization of modern man's philosophy. Thus Marxism helped to eliminate religion by substituting the false promise of an earthly Utopia for it. God was exiled by middle-class liberal philosophy and was replaced by a man-made doctrine which holds the greatest danger for the middle class itself.

The success of Marxism lies above all in the fact that no spiritual forces were at hand to take up its challenge. Middle class philosophy ruined the forces which would have resisted the corroding effect of Marxism. Man's philosophy was despiritualized. However, Marxist philosophy is just as materialistic as is the liberal philosophy to which it is closely tied by bonds of Hegelian concepts and methods. It is also unrealistic, just as liberal philosophy is unrealistic. Both disregard man's sinful nature. This is clear enough if we think of the Utopian character of the Communist society as depicted by Marx.

The twentieth century, in spite of all the implications of both liberalism and socialism as to man's "essential goodness" and his perfectibility, did not bring the awaited and predicted happiness through a perfect world for all. It brought disillusionment, wars, and disgust. It also brought the long overdue revolt against reason in the camp of the philosophers. This philosopher's revolt did not clear the atmosphere. Man lost faith in his own reason, but the new speculations of contemporary thinkers and social scientists confused the present even more. Nor did it do anything to clear the way for a reasonable solution of man's most important material problems: war and poverty.

The new science of psychology began to tamper with something which until then had been untouched by modern scientists. Man's soul became the plaything of this field of study, the cultivators of which taught that the primary motive behind man's action was not reason but instinct. They thought that reason was only the instrument by which man's impulses seek their satisfaction. With this vogue man, as the exalted "rational animal" of an earlier era, was dethroned and a rather pitiful and dependent creature of instinct took its place.

The revolt against reason went so far that the very irrationality of man became the foundation on which new theories were built to explain the action of mankind. The most dramatic philosopher in this revolt was the German Nietzsche who, after declaring the death of God, went on to proclaim the advent of the superman as the incarnation of "the will to power." This hectic chase for empty ideas ended with the last cry in modern thought: existentialism, a philosophy of despair expressing the bottomless anguish and distress of modern man.

A last word has to be added to this rapid journey through the jungle of modern man's philosophical thought. As our days become acceleratingly hectic, so does man's thought. During the last fifty years or so man has jumped from one theory to another to explain life, to give reasons for his own existence, and to devise a goal for which to live. However, in spite of the terrific nervous tension, in spite of the hectic pace, none of the fundamental problems of life's secrets have been solved.

The great questions of life cannot be solved without belief in harmonizing values. They cannot be solved if spirit is not considered. The problems of existence will always trouble and haunt man and will be left unsolved until man will base his approach to them on eternal, transcending values and thus will be enabled to fit his problems into a greater universal whole. They are never solved satisfactorily without the help of God. Only the God revealed by Jesus Christ is the true God.

37

Not until we have reassured ourselves about the meaning of life can we turn towards the solution of our earthly problems. The vital question of war, misery, and exploitation of man by man, can be solved only if modern man restores God in the temple of his heart. With God's help man will be able to apply spiritual values to the solution of the great practical problems of man's survival in the atomic age.

Some signs exist that the despiritualization of man's thought, if not the despiritualization of his life, has been arrested. Great living thinkers are modest enough to recognize finally that man's only salvation consists in his return to God. They believe that man can only avoid the dreaded catastrophe on this earth if he lets his steps be directed by Christianity.

---

* For more details about Western man's political thinking the reader is referred to the following two excellent books: MAIN CURRENTS IN MODERN POLITICAL THOUGHT by John H. Hallowell and A HISTORY OF POLITICAL THEORY by George H. Sabine.

PART TWO

CHAPTER II

THE CYCLICAL THEORY OF SPENGLER
AND ITS REFUTATION

In the first chapter we observed the growing inter-dependence of the nations of the world. The peace, the well-being and the freedom of each nation has become dependent on the peace, well-being, and the freedom of the rest of the nations. No nation can have security, prosperity, and liberty alone in this interdependent world. While the interdependence of all nations calls for international solution, mankind is still divided into sovereign nation-states, which seem to be unable to organize themselves into a universal political organization capable of solving the common problems of all.

We also observed that the unsolved problems of war and human misery have engendered doctrines offering false and dangerous solutions. The false prophets of Bolshevik-communism correctly saw the symptoms of the ailment of the sickened world in war and misery. However, being obsessed with materialistic considerations they could not rightly diagnose the malady itself. They could not find the fundamental cause of the crisis of our troubled world: spiritual stagnation.

We have also considered briefly the ultimate cause of Western man's inability to solve the problem of international organization and of his failure to win over false doctrines. We have found the cause in the fact that modern philosophy and social science have gradually eliminated all spiritual considerations. Spiritual inspirations, needed even for the solution of worldly problems, have not been forth-coming. The core of modern man's tragedy is the despirit-ualization of his thought and life. Now, when he needs higher inspiration to win over his national-egoistic inclinations in his struggles to build a political world community,

41

he does not have it. Now, when he needs spiritual weapons to win over false doctrines, he lacks them.

The rest of this book will be devoted to the examination of the problem of whether man has a chance to establish an institutionalized world community. This task, of necessity, will involve a search for the kind of spiritual inspiration that is needed to enable man to overcome the retrograde forces of ultra-nationalism and to fight off the temptation of Marxist Communism.

To carry out this plan we will analyse a particular theory of history which well represents modern materialistic thinking. We propose to take a look at the cyclical theory as propounded by its best known advocate, Oswald Spengler, German philosopher of history. While it is true that we picked his theory as our target to prove our point, this is not because we overestimate his importance. We are aware of the fact that he was only the product of his time and only one of the many philosophers who, as a whole, led man's thinking to its present dangerous state. However, since, in the field of philosophy of history, his cyclical theory can be considered as the last chapter of a tragic trend of thinking, and since his sinister conclusions are the logical result of a long prevailing materialistic philosophy, and especially since his theory implies the impossibility of world organization, we chose his idea as our target. Our argument is with materialistic thinking in general and not with Spenglerism in particular. By trying to refute the Spenglerian theory we aim at the whole structure of materialistic thinking, as we must if we want to clear the way toward the acceptance of a purposeful international organization.

We are sure that man cannot win the fight for an organized world community and cannot be victorious over the false doctrines of our times unless he gives up materialistic philosophy and reaffirms the primacy of spirituality in the realm of thought and action. The advocates of the cyclical theory look at mankind—as do materialistic thinkers in general—as an aimlessly drifting plaything placed in the hands of unknown fatal forces immanent in matter and ruled by the laws of evolution. They substitute an artificially created, imaginary, and supposedly self-regulating, author-

42

less "order" for God. While they cannot explain the great problems of existence, they destroy man's faith in his Creator and rob him of his belief in a higher destiny.

The advocates of the cyclical theory deal with man's history in terms of separate individual civilizations, which they compare to the organisms of the physical world. According to them, every civilization follows certain unexplained rules, fixed in advance by an aimless destiny. These immanent rules limit the existence of each and every civilization to a predestined life-span. This life expectancy can be expressed in a fixed number of years. The believers in this theory depict the individual civilizations as self-sufficient and independent units. After running the full course of its allotted life-span, each of them is submerged without influencing later civilizations. Everything has to start all over again. History expresses itself in cycles. No progress exists. Civilizations rise, flourish, and fall. Western civilization is not exempted from this general order of hopelessness. It is also doomed to perish. Just as the physical laws of any living organism apply without exception to each unit of the species, so the immanent laws of civilizations apply to each historic culture.

It is not surprising that our age of materialism has brought forth such a pessimistic view of man's history. It is no wonder that this faithless age sees no promise in the future. Matter has become the supreme value. For materialistic philosophy nothing else exists but matter and man himself is nothing but matter. Spenglerism is the logical result of the complete despiritualization of human thinking. The historian of a despiritualized age could not explain man's history in any terms except in terms of materialism.

It is necessary to deal with the cyclical theory in detail because by implication, it denies the possibility of the progressive unification of mankind. By this denial it robs man of faith in the coming of a universal organization and thus weakens his will to work for a safer and better future. What this theory represents is spiritual nihilism and this, in turn, is at the core of the negative attitude of those who deny the possibility of a more progressive international order. We repudiate the assumption of predestined aimlessness and global doom. Born in the despair of ignorance about human destiny, this theory of gloom denies the very idea of progress. We reject this idea of frustration based on materialistic philosophy. Accepting it would mean that there is no way out of the present international anarchy. Believing in it would mean to give up all hope of creating a better organized and a better governed international community. It would mean recognizing defeat in the struggle for the elimination of war and for the establishment of world peace.

In order to satisfy ourselves that institutionalized, international co-operation and world-wide political integration are not beyond all hope, we must examine and if possible, refute the assertions and implications of Spengler-minded thinkers. What are, then, the assertions and implications of the cyclical theory which, if accepted would definitely discourage us from believing in the possibility of human progress in general and in institutionalized peaceful international relations in particular?

1. The largest human collective units through which history reveals itself are the different individual civilizations. This assertion denies the fundamental oneness of the human race.

2. The civilizations of the different regions of the world and of the different ages of history are organic units with a predetermined, immanent life-span fixed in a limited number of years. They live out their given and restricted possibilities uninfluenced by the preceding or neighboring civilizations. This assertion of Spengler denies the interdependence of the different civilizations.

3. Since all civilizations are organism-like units, they inevitably come to an end. With each new civilization there is a completely new start. Civilizations come and go without any ultimate forward movement. History pulsates in ever-repeating cycles. The cyclical theory denies progress.

4. The Spenglerians do not discern any difference between our modern civilization and the preceding civilizations. All particular civilizations are doomed to fail. They do not only imply but they predict the downfall of the West-civilization.

44

5. All these assertions naturally imply the impossibility of more advanced political integration in the international field.

In summary, here are the five important implications of the cyclical theory which we desire to refute:

1. The denial of the oneness of the human race.
2. The negation of the interdependence of the different civilization.
3. The denial of human progress.
4. The prediction of the downfall of our Western civilization.
5. The denial of a coming better world brought about by the political integration of the human race.

Those who have no faith in the eventual establishment of an institutionalized, peaceful co-operation of all nations knowingly or unknowingly use the above stated assertions and implications of Spenglerian philosophy in their effort to prove that man never will be able to surmount the difficulties which stand in the way of the creation of an internationally ordered world.

Let us now, therefore, proceed and discuss the implications of the Spenglerian theories point by point and refute them—if we can—by facts derived from a study of history.

1. RACE THEORY OR THE ONENESS
OF THE HUMAN RACE?

If any fact is significant for an understanding of the shape of things to come, it is the opening of all the corners of the world for intercommunication and the subsequent intermingling of all races. This has been a gradual process which started with the progressive development of the several media of communication and transportation. The modern intermingling of races, brought about by the West, goes back to the time of the great discoveries of faraway lands by the white man. These led him to settle in great numbers in the newly discovered territories and to live and die among the natives he encountered there. The racial situation of the colonies was made more complex in cases such as that of the Western Hemisphere, where the scarcity of the Indian population or the inability or unwillingness of the natives to work induced the white settlers to import Negro slaves by the shiploads from Africa. A new wave of migration set in, in which the participants were unwilling objects and were meant to serve the predatory instinct of the white man.

The mass migration of modern times was further spurred by the coming of the Industrial Revolution. The industrialization of certain countries started a flow of labor from the agricultural countries to the industrialized ones. This helped to build up the population of such countries as the United States. However, at this stage the white masters of the "new countries" mostly limited immigration to the white race since they were not too anxious to let the non-white into the sparsely populated new lands in spite of the pathetic desire of the Asians to relieve the population pressure of their own countries. Not only did the United States adopt immigration measures discriminating against Asians; Canada, Australia, and New Zealand did the same. Consequently the main stream of the later colored migration could flow only to the colonial territories of Asia, Africa, Oceania, and in some cases also to the Caribbean region controlled by European powers. The sons and daughters of overpopulated China, Japan, India, and Indonesia were those who contributed mostly to this relatively recent migration which further changed the racial mosaic of the world. This last mentioned migration accounts substantially for the very mixed racial background of some Asian (chiefly Southeast Asian), African and (to a lesser extent) Latin American countries.

The political and economic upheavals of our own days have further added to the more or less constant flow of immigrants leaving their respective countries in search of a better life, more safety, or even mere survival.

As the result of mass-migration in many countries of the world several races are by now living side by side in permanent residence. Besides this type of permanent connection between different races, which results from settlement of immigrants in foreign countries, there are many opportunities which offer transitory contact between the representatives of the different races in the several fields of human endeavor. These contacts are made ever easier as they are stimulated by the rapidly developing facilities of modern travel. Foreign trade is one important factor connecting nations and races and leading to close personal relations between their representatives. Bilateral diplomacy has always provided many opportunities to bring together people of different nations and races. Its field of activity, and the personal contact it furthers, is becoming ever more important. The multiplication of international political forums in our day offers more and more opportunities for races to meet. One has only to think of the periodical meetings of the several organs of the United Nations, especially that of the General Assembly, which bring representatives of practically all nations and races intimately together for many months each year. The universities offer a meeting place for young men and women of different racial background. Ventures of scientific and cultural exchange, such as international conferences, likewise bring together people of the same interest, though of different color. Even inter-

47

national sports events can play an important role in bringing nations and races together.

Both the permanent settlement of immigrants in foreign countries and the multiplying types of transitory contacts of the representatives of different races give many opportunities to observe the similarities of the several branches of the human race. The unbiased and open-minded observer of our day must be profoundly struck by how much we all— white, black, and yellow—are alike.

It is, indeed, a tragic testimony to the narrowness of the human mind, that even in this time of modern racial inter-mingling, which has been going on ever since the sixteenth century, and in the face of multiplying evidences to the contrary, thinkers such as Count Gobineau, Houston Stewart Chamberlain and in our own country Professor Burgess could advocate the superiority of the Caucasian race and stand for racial discrimination. Evil fruits of such thinking have not been slow to ripen. Naziism, with its racial perse-cutions, was the result.

In the following pages we will list some evidences which, in our mind, are weighty enough to substantiate our deep conviction about the essential unity of the human race.

1. Biologically, mankind is one sole, indivisible unit. The outstanding biological proof of the oneness of the human race is the fact that individuals of all races can interbreed and can raise healthy, normal children. Evidences were already cited by Darwin in his *The Origin of Species and The Descent of Man* to the effect that all human races are descendants of the same stock.

The great number of the light-colored United States Negroes "passing over" into the American white community is an excellent illustration of the oneness of the human race. According to expert estimates, every year around 10,000 light skinned Negroes find their way into the white population. The number of those who have passed over since the Civil War is put as high as one and a half million. Their descendants, in by far the most cases, do not know about their mixed ancestry. It is also estimated that, con-sidering the great number of light-skinned Negroes who have passed over from the Negro to the white community, there may be about 10,000,000 Americans with a drop or two of black blood, without knowing it. While this number seems to be exaggerated, there is no doubt that "passings" occur in great number.

2. While anthropologists do not all agree on this, most authorities believe that the human race originated from a common homeland. Darwin himself thought that man spread slowly from his original common birthplace over the earth. The hypothesis that places the original home of the human race in Central-Asia seems to be the most generally accepted. Pressure of population (which comes early among hunting people) and the thrill of adventure subsequently drove migrating groups into all directions to populate eventually the whole world. This brought the so-called separate races into existence. Not even Darwin believed in the separate origin of the races.

3. Emotional drives, according to psychologists, motivate man's actions. The desire to dominate, to forge ahead, to get rich, to please our fellowmen, to be admired, and so on, are said to dominate human life. While we do not think that emotional factors are the only ones which explain man's actions, and while we deny that man is only an emotional creature, we do recognize the great influence that man's emotional life plays in history. Since our purpose is to prove human unity and the oneness of the human race, it is necessary to state that there is no notable difference in the emotional life of men of different races. The so-called human drives are the same among all of us. They have the same power over the members of the differently colored human groups.

4. Neither can one see any difference between the races as far as intellectual capacities are concerned. The achievements of the non-white civilizations are far from being inferior to what the white man produced prior to Christianity. It is with the deepest respect that we consider the grandeur of the Egyptian, Chaldean, or Inca civilization. Nor have we any right to feel superior to our contemporary Chinese or Indian fellowmen. The intellectual achievements and the material creations of non-white men are the best proof that intellectually they are our full equals. We

49

cannot but appreciate the knowledge they have passed on to us when we recognize that our civilization is based on the foundation built by peoples of non-Caucasian origin.

The high quality of the intellectual achievements of the non-white races is not the only witness to the similarities in intellectual ability of white and colored peoples. It is intriguing to study historical evidences proving how co-existing but not necessarily intercommunicating civilizations followed the same line of intellectual development, often under completely different circumstances. Sometimes even specific discoveries were made at approximately the same time by civilizations far removed from each other without any traces of preparatory interchange. Man's mind works the same way, whether he is white or yellow. Similar mental processes bring similar results. The undeniable mental affinity of the human races also points to the same origin and oneness of mankind.

5. Further proof of the oneness of the human race is the fact that so-called primitive races easily can adopt (practically without any intermediary stages) the ways of a higher type of civilization. For instance, it is uplifting to observe how the American Negro is adapting himself to the ways of the highly civilized life now prevailing in the United States. In the span of a few generations the former slaves, that is, their children and children's children, were able to lift their cultural standard almost to the level of their American surroundings. They produced men and women of outstanding intellectual and spiritual abilities. Actually their innate intellectual, spiritual, as well as physical capacities are like those of the white man. The situation is fundamentally the same in the former colonial territories of Asia and Africa as it is also in the lands which are still under the rule of the white man. Already during the paternalistic period of colonialism great strides were made in intellectual and material advancement of the subjected peoples. Colonial peoples, in spite of all handicaps, were fully able to live up to the requirements of Western cultural standards.

Furthermore, the newly emancipated non-white nations are about to demonstrate that they can take care of themselves politically as well as white people can. They are fully capable of self-government and able to make up their own minds as to what they need and how they are going to achieve it. They are equal partners in the present nation-state system, not only legally, but also in ability to play the same role as the older members of the community of nations are playing. They might even be able to help in finding a way out of the present impasse of international relations.

6. Nor is the spiritual make-up of the different races at variance. Man's moral values are not different according to the color of his skin. If they are different it is not because of the difference in color. They all have the innate capacity to differentiate between good and bad. This does not necessarily mean that man always is listening to the voice of his conscience. Hideous practices born of false social and political concepts might prevail for a long time in some civilizations. These misusages are only temporarily deforming man's soul. Despite all the pagan practices and abuses prevailing in pre-Christian and non-Christian societies, the divine spark never was completely extinguished in their souls. Under the surface of their foul outside behavior, despite all aberrations, hidden but ready to regerminate at the first contact with wholesome influence, man's inborn conscience is patiently awaiting the time when it can take over the direction of his actions. The voice of man's conscience is alike in the members of all races.

As the so-called Law of Nature implies, the fundamental moral conceptions are alike in all epochs and in all regions. They are common to all peoples and races. They are universal and eternal. Such ideas as to be good to our fellow-man if we expect good from him; or not to misuse the weakness of the children and the old; or to be hospitable to one's guest; and similar norms are generally accepted by all races. If, however, moral ideals are forgotten in a certain land or at a certain epoch, it would be completely unfair to tag the blame on that particular race. All races alike are exposed to the temptation of the flesh. Sin is not confined to a race. Man is born with sin irrespective of the color of the skin. Our own Western civilization was

51

just as much marred by foul practices as were the rest of human civilizations.

In order to strengthen the voice of our conscience, man needs to be fully aware of the commands of the Law of Nature. The uncultivated conscience of the individual is too weak to fight temptation. We have to cultivate our moral gifts just as we have to train our physical organs, lest they degenerate. Men of all races needed the guidance of religion and aspired the consolation which only faith can give.

The problem of what happens to man after death has haunted him since he became conscious of his existence. The duality of man—that he is both spirit and matter—is recognized by the most primitive as well as by the most advanced peoples. It is probably the most tragic feature of our modern culture that this most elementary fact has been overlooked, even by many scholars of great repute and merit. In this respect their stand is unscientific and it disregards the teaching of history. How can we deny the existence of spirit when we are reminded of it at every moment by death itself?

Man was always intrigued by the mystery of human existence. Throughout history all races have been concerned with and excited over this problem. Man himself is the mystery of mysteries, which he never will be able to explain by rational means. Only one explanation proved to be satisfactory everywhere and in all ages: man could only be explained in terms of his Creator, God. According to all religious beliefs, the ultimate solution of the "why" of human existence dwells outside of the limited confines of the material world.

The oneness of mankind cannot be better proved than by faith in God. All roads of human thought and all speculations finally converge on God. We are all members of the same human family, because we are all created by the same God. The religions embraced by the different racial groups all express the great desire of man to know himself by knowing God.

7. A further proof of the oneness of mankind is the fact that economic, social, and political institutions showed the

same pattern of development in all regions of the world and through all ages. Not even the most geographically isolated civilizations are exceptions to this general rule. Neither can those countries be excepted which tried artificially to isolate themselves from the rest of the world by severing all connections with the outside. Social, economic, and political institutions show a remarkable resemblance in all ages and regions, irrespective of color, race, or creed of the people concerned. Geographically separated groups of the common human stock always reacted alike to similar stimuli and found the same solutions to the same problems. Let us first take a look at some aspects of the common economic pattern.

The material existence of man in all times and in all lands depended ultimately on the land. Aspects of the economic well-being of settled population were intimately tied up with the different ways of land ownership. The same gradual evolution of ownership can be observed by historians all over the world and among all races. The tribal ownership gave way only slowly to family-owned land, and it was only after long development that private property of the land as we know it today was recognized. Ownership or possession of land meant not only more security and a more pleasant life for the family, but it also became the measure of the social and political standing of the owner. It is interesting to observe how feudalism arose in all nations, how it developed the same characteristics all over the world, and how it brought about like institutions everywhere. It was not only in Europe that feudalism dominated nearly all fields of human endeavor during long centuries, but it also pervaded most aspects of human life in such countries as Japan, China, India, as well as in the rest of Asia. The same exploitation of the miserable serfs prevailed in Asia as it did many thousands of miles away in Europe and Africa.

The oppressive land-tenure system became the foundation of the feudal state all over the world. Ranks were distributed, and constitutional positions were attained in accordance with the power emanating from the size and fertility of the land controlled. With the rise of city civilization, land owners all over the world were attracted to cities, and thus absentee landlordism became the common plague of all agricultural countries. Wherever the historian looks, the same dismal picture of the contrast between the misery-ridden peasant masses and the luxury-living landlords confronts him. The problem of destitution of hundreds of millions of miserable serfs and the question of how to satisfy the legitimate need of the abused and exploited peasantry for land still loomed large on the horizon in the great majority of the countries of the globe when the Twentieth Century dawned. This problem still remains unsolved in some places.

The rise of the merchant class with progressively enlarging trading radius also follows the same pattern all over the world. Neither does the technique of monetary economy differ essentially in terms of the various regions of the world. Merchant and artisan classes followed similar practices to become rich. Nowhere were they shy to charge exorbitant interest on money lent to the needy. At important points of communication on the land and along the seas, they built cities all over the globe according to the same pattern. They developed world-trade and started intercontinental navigation.

Men all over the world, in all ages, without any difference of races, faced the same problems of livelihood. In the process of survival they resorted to the same solutions. The same economic habits were practiced and the same economic institutions sprung up everywhere.

8. To dominate and to exploit, to misuse the weakness of lower classes, is a general human characteristic when higher inspirations do not counteract this drive. The result is class differentiation everywhere. The measure of discrimination may vary; however, they have existed and still do exist in all parts of the world and among all races. They still plague mankind. Not even Christianity succeeded in eradicating social discrimination and building communities based on social equality. The ways of setting up class barriers are strikingly similar in all regions. This is further testimony to the fundamental oneness of the human race.

Slavery was also common to all nations, regions, and

civilizations.   Not alone the non-Western countries em
braced it. Not only the glory of ancient Greece was marred
by it.   The so-called Christian countries were not exempt
from this shame.   It took a long time to eradicate this
institution, the memory of which is still haunting us.

9. Neither is it surprising that man's political behavior is
alike among all races. As the fundamental disposition of the
members of the human race are the same, they all follow
the same political pattern while encountering the same problems of politics.

Clans and tribes, based on blood relationship, form the
first type of political organization everywhere. This form of
political community is still alive in many parts of Asia and
Africa. There are even territories in Europe where this type
of political organization survives, for instance in Albania.
At a very early stage of human civilization, at the crossroads
of land and sea communication, city-states emerged. They
grew not only on the shores of the Mediterranean, but also
in Central-Asia, on the China Sea, along the great rivers of
Asia-Minor, and on the Indian subcontinent. The inhabitants
of these city-states (no matter whether they belonged to the
Caucasian, Mongol, Semitic, Hamitic races) being stimulated
by the exchange of material and spiritual values, produced
brilliant cultures of everlasting importance. Simultaneously,
or as the next step of political organization, neighboring or
related tribes were brought under the domination of a strong
leader, the king. Kingdoms arose all over the world. The
most powerful of them sought to extend their power. Empires
of regional or even world fame came into being. This was
also common to all the regions of the world. The pattern
of empire building was very much the same in the cases of
Alexander, Caesar, Genghis Khan, Suleiman, or the Arab
kalifs. All the races and regions gave empire builders to the
world.

The above nine points should amply illustrate our contention that it is illusory to talk about the so-called individual
races as separate, independent groups, having no connection
to each other. In the true sense of the word, only one human
race exists. Mankind is an integral, natural unit. The facts
prove Christianity's teaching about the oneness of the
human race.

2. *REGIONAL OR UNIVERSAL CIVILIZATION?*

The Spenglerians think in terms of isolated individual civilizations, as though no intercommunication existed between the civilizations of the great regions of the world. They look at the civilizations of the ancient Egyptians, Sumerians, Greeks, and Romans as though they followed the rules of living organism with predetermined life-span and without essential dependence on each other. They think of the regional civilizations as organism-like units which are pre-destined to fall and leave nothing behind them from which the following civilizations could profit.

In the preceding part of this chapter, on the basis of a study of history, we argued for the essential oneness of mankind. From the acceptance of the fact of human oneness follows the rejection of that part of Spenglerian theory which implies the denial of the interdependence of the great individual civilizations. If essentially there is only one mankind, there must also be an essentially indivisible human civilization that transcends all times and all regions. What we consider individual regional civilizations are parts of one universal civilization. They cannot be viewed as existing independent of each other.

While, thus, the oneness of the human race alone should be sufficient to disprove the theory of self motivated and independently existing civilizations, we propose to substantiate further our belief that the great regional civilizations never lived completely separated, but that sparse contacts existed between them.

Complete physical isolation could not have been possible if for no other reason than the oneness of the globe, its physical unity, and its uninterrupted continuity. All races can live in all parts of the world. They can penetrate all corners of the globe. No individual race can permanently separate or isolate itself. Where one human group can go, the other can follow. There is no place to hide from each other in a closed world.

Modern man is tempted to underestimate the abilities of his fellow-man of an earlier epoch. We are too proud of our technological progress and are apt to think that in time of primitive communication the different human groups lived separated because they did not have the means we have now to contact and visit each other. We depend too much on our gadgets and our machines and it is hard for us to imagine that without technology man could master the great problem of inter-regional communication. But while in terms of time our advance in communication is impressive, in terms of space our human ancestors, considering all their disadvantages, did very well indeed.

If we believe that man before our age could not travel far and could not inter-communicate in the regional sense, we will too readily give credence to those who deny the interdependence of the regional civilizations. So that we may not commit this mistake, it will help to take a look at the mobility of pre-modern man and his relation to the problem of distance.

In times of primitive communication, though physical hindrances seemed immense they were not prohibitive. During the pre-historic migrations which led man from his original common home to all corners of the globe, his mobility was assured by the domestication of transport animals. Even after the original "emigrants" reached the farthest corners of the world, fairly regular communication must have existed between the different regions. Nomadic ways must have survived for a long time. Transport animals and primitive conveyances assured intercommunication between the dispersed groups of the same human race.

Thus the American Indian roamed all over the North American continent in search of a happy hunting ground. Archeologists seem to be certain that tribal wanderings must have been going on for thousands of years between Asia and North America through the Aleutian lands. By island hopping the Mongoloid tribes of Asia and America kept in contact for a long time. The equestrian nomads of Asia were also continuously on the go. We must marvel at the relative ease with which they overcame the immense distances of the Eurasian steppes. They covered thousands of miles each year by riding on the backs of their horses.

Only with the rise of predominantly sedentary agricultural civilizations did this picture of easy intercommunication begin to change. The first great attempt of man to overcome distances and to penetrate all corners of the globe came to an end when no pastures remained undiscovered. From the nomadic point of view the world became overpopulated. The consequent population pressure compelled man to try to extract from the soil more products than it offered of itself. Man settled down to farming. The settled part of the population soon forgot the art of mobility as transport animals were used to break up the virgin soil. Man could dispense with mobility, since his sedentary occupation attached him to the soil. Stability was forced on man when he had to wait while the crop ripened and became ready for harvesting. The transportation of the rather bulky crop, on which he now depended for survival, was beyond the means of primitive technique. This also compelled man to stay put.

However, because the change to a more sedentary life was not general, nomadic ways survived for many millennia. This was especially the case where vast open spaces such as the steppe lands of Eurasia or the rugged tablelands of Central Asia favored the ways of warrior nomads. It is not surprising that, while primitive kingdoms covering small, usually well sheltered territories were generally established by farmers, some of the most important so-called world empires were built by nomads who retained the art of mobility and the roughness required to fight and conquer. Thanks to their greater mobility, they could better control immense territories. The territorially greatest empire which ever existed was built in the late Middle Ages in an epoch predominantly sedentary as far as the West was concerned. Genghis Khan and the Golden Horde controlled greater territories than the largest land-power, the Soviet Union, does today.

The more sedentary life of primitive farming facilitated the accumulation of wealth. It made storage possible. Agricultural communities became richer. They developed primitive artisanship and trades. Since they lived a more sheltered life, they were the first to develop culture. However, the big stimulus came from the exchange of material and spiritual values among the different groups. The merchants became a class in themselves and gradually attained

58

an important position in history. With them the problem was, again, how to master mobility and how to overcome the obstacle of space. They developed shipping and founded colonies. They sailed all the oceans and contacted peoples of different civilizations. True, their overseas journeys were time consuming, but they could cover just as great distances as men could in later ages. Besides becoming rich they also acquired knowledge by visiting foreign lands and observing the ways of other peoples. It is not surprising that some merchant republics, due to such accumulation of wealth and knowledge, grew into immense empires. The greatest stimulus possible, that of learning how different peoples solve similar problems, helped them on their way to success. Rome was not the only empire built by a city-state.

Today we live in an epoch of extreme mobility. Physical distances are shrinking in terms of time because of the newly-developed means of communication. Man begins to think about stratospheric communication and about travel in space. However, as a matter of fact, man always has been able to solve the problems of regional communication and always has been able to face up to the necessities posed by spatial separation. This was especially the case with the nomads and the merchant class.

It is not only pre-modern man's ability to communicate and overcome global distances that supports our contention that the separated parts of the same human race never lost complete contact with each other. Specific historic instances also prove the reality of intercommunication of historic civilizations.

As intellectual connections among all regions and civilizations are intensified in our times, as scholars are given access to hidden, forgotten documents in all parts of the world, as archeological research and the results of excavations bring more and more light to the study of history, a fascinating picture of intermingling early civilizations begins to unfold.

Let us look now at some specific historic instances to further illustrate our belief that regional civilizations never ceased to intercommunicate.

The Near East, including the Nile Valley and Mesopotamia, is called the cradle of civilization. While this region is only the cradle of Western civilization, the past achievements of its peoples are glorious enough to make them proud. The brilliance of the culture of the ancient Near East is due, in great measure, to the fact that this region is situated at the crossroad of the different regional civilizations. I mention only two facts of paramount importance here. First, the flow of our civilization led through this region. Second, this region acted as a connecting link between the nations of the Far East and the peoples of the Helleno-Roman civilization.

About the intermixture of all the related Mediterranean civilizations there can hardly be any doubt. It is fascinating to study the intermingling of the ancient culture of the Egyptians and the other nations of the Near East. It is hardly possible to separate the interlinking cultural roots of the peoples of the Mediterranean region. They all owe so much to each other. They have all shared in the great accomplishment of the Hellenic world. They all contributed to build imperial Rome. The human base of Christian civilization is manifold. Christianity itself is rooted in this fertile soil. Not only the sea-lanes were kept open by such seafaring nations as the Phoenicians, Carthaginians, Hellenes, and Romans, but also land routes connected the nations of these regions.

This interdependence and the exchange in merchandise and spirit did not end with the rise of the two foremost religions of the region—Christianity and Mohammedanism. Although the two fought each other on the field of battle, they could not help but profoundly influence each other. While the direct flow of Western civilization led through the Greek peninsula, in more than one instance the ancient Hellenic heritage itself was transferred to the Christian West indirectly through contemporary Arab sources. Such was the case with the works of Aristotle, who after having been forgotten in Europe, became known again to the Western world by Arabic translation. After the fall of the Roman Empire, while the uneasy West suffered the assaults of the barbarian Germanic tribes, it was the Arab world which was the chief upholder of progress.

Neither can we accept the view that the Far East and India represent a civilization of their own. India was always connected with the Near East and indirectly with the West.

60

Since the early Aryan invasion around 2000 B.C. India has been hit in waves by invaders coming from the West through the northwest passes. Aryans, and later Moslem-Mongols brought their own ways to India and in turn accepted the native Indian customs. The interchange between India and the Near East was continuous. Indians reached Arabia and even Egypt. They also traded with the Roman Empire. India was not beyond the imagination of Western Europeans. Nor was India isolated from what was to the East of her. Her culture had been spreading eastward as far as ancient Cambodia. The southeastern nations of Asia also were connected with India by navigation and trade. Indian influence reached what is modern-day Indonesia. We know of early Chinese travelers who visited India, the birthplace of Gautama, founder of Buddhism, and Buddhism itself spread from India to China and Japan.

Ever since the beginning of recorded history, connections have existed between the West and the Far East. At the beginning of the Christian era, overland routes were used between China and the Roman Empire for importation of Chinese silk. This route led through Central Asia, known as Turkestan. Ancient cities, such as Samarkand, Lopnor, and Kashgar, attest to the importance of this early Western-Chinese trade. It is also a historic fact that the Christian religion penetrated into China at an early age. The Nestorian missionaries reached China through India and Central Asia in the seventh century A.D. and built churches for their Chinese converts. This early Chinese-Christian church survived two centuries. We also know that in the later Middle Ages Christian Europe, under the spiritual leadership of the Pope, was successful in establishing direct connection with China, then part of the Mongol Empire. Christian envoys were sent by the Pope to the court of the Great Khan to talk over plans for the conversion of his subjects in the thirteenth century. Louis IX of France also sent emisarries to the camp of Genghis Khan in Mongolia to secure an alliance against the menacing onslaught of the Mohammedans. The best-known early connection between Western Europe and the Far East was brought about by the two Venetian merchants Nicola and Maffeo Polo. They were received around 1264 by Kublai

Khan in his capital at Cambaluc (modern Peking). It was Marco Polo, Nicola's son, himself a merchant traveler and visitor in the Khan's camp, who gave literary expression to these early China connections. He was also the first Western man to mention Zipanga (Japan). The sixteenth-century story of the Catholic mission under Matico Ricci, in China, is a matter of recent history.

To demonstrate the roundabout ways by which human knowledge is sometimes transferred, we note that the first Western information about China stems from Turkish sources, which were used by Byzantine writers and taken over by Western authors.

Considerable foreign trade was carried on between China and Moslem Arabia beginning in the tenth century. Arabs were permitted to settle in China and take Chinese wives, a privilege very surprising in view of Chinese reluctance to permit Western traders in the first part of the nineteenth century even to stay overnight within the walls of Canton.

All this proves that the expression "discovery," as applied to the exploits of Vasco da Gama and his successors in the sixteenth century, is misleading. China did not have to be discovered. Land communication existed long before the Portuguese navigators set out on their eastward voyage and landed on the Spice Islands.

Not even the Western hemisphere was isolated from the rest of the world. Evidences are multiplying—as we stated before—to prove that intercommunication existed between Asia and the Western Hemisphere for many millennia prior to Columbus' coming to America. When, later, this inter-continental movement slowed down and finally ceased, the atrophy of the population was such that when the white man appeared on the scene the native did not have the stamina to fight back and to withstand the corrupting influence of the invader. The degeneration was due to lack of invigorating influence from outside.

We also know now that to refer to Columbus as the discoverer of America is hardly correct. This is incorrect, even if we look at the problem from the purely European point of view. Columbus was far from the first European to set foot on American soil. Norsemen reached the shores of this continent at least five centuries before Columbus did.

The above historic illustrations are given to prove that connections existed among civilizations and that trade and cultural exchange was carried on. They were taken at random and do not exhaust the recorded connections between civilizations. Besides, innumerable documents recording such contacts have been destroyed by natural disasters and wars. Many known facts were forgotten. There also must have been countless unrecorded connections.

On the basis of our limited number of illustrations, we can repeat that the different regional civilizations never lived in complete isolation. Men of different civilizations and of different regions knew about each other. They exchanged ideas and products. They traded goods and knowledge. While it is certainly true that their fundamental similarity can be explained by the fact of the oneness of the human race, it is also true that connections between the different regions account for specific similarities.

No completely independent civilization has ever existed. All the known civilizations have interlocked in one way or another; in some cases directly, in others indirectly. They have influenced each other even if this influence was hardly noticeable. The regional civilizations have intercommunicated not only in time, but also in space. Not only have succeeding civilizations built on the heritage of preceding ones, but the geographically separated, contemporaneous civilizations have also profited from each other's achievements.

In the broad sense, there is only one civilization—the integral civilization of the whole human race. In the final analysis, national and regional civilizations are only interdependent branches of the all-embracing civilization of the one human race.

With the coming of modern navigation, and especially with the development of the Industrial Revolution, the rather sparse contacts of the past have been succeeded by an intense and ever more rapidly developing international interdependence affecting all parts of the human race. Today this means much more than economic interdependence. We will take up this problem in detail in a later chapter.

3. CYCLES OR PROGRESS?

Possibly the most disturbing implication of the cyclical theory is the suggestion that mankind marches in a circle, that no progress exists, that man travels in a blind alley which does not lead anywhere.

This conclusion follows from the main premise on which this theory is built. The premise asserts that the human race is divided into supposedly self-sufficient compartments of regional civilizations, and the conclusion follows that because the individual civilizations fall there is no progress. The premise disregards the unity of mankind. It explains history in terms of regional civilizations, which it likens to isolated organism-like units.

But is it not arbitrary and unscholarly to take apart things which belong together? Will our vision not be blurred, will our judgment not err if we artificially separate parts of the same unit and endow them with separate existence? How can we expect general human progress, if we think only in terms of different races and regions? What the cyclicalists do is like cutting off all the branches of the same living tree, and then pretending that the severed branches are independent trees. Their mistake is to apply their observations about the dead branches to a living tree.

We, indeed, have reason to become desperate if we look only at the separate histories of the individual nations or of the individual civilizations. The picture mirrored in their history rightly disconcerts us. However, we are not entitled to draw hasty conclusions from the fate of the parts. The nations and the regional civilizations are parts of the great entity of the whole human race. We should refrain from drawing any conclusion until we consider the entire picture, that of the whole of humankind.

If we consider only the individual races, regions and civilizations apart from the whole, we shall not be qualified to answer the question of whether there is or is not a progressive forward march in human history, nor shall we be in a position to tell whether progress exists or whether mankind is marching in a circle. Judging from the narrow perspective of regional civilizations, we cannot decide whether in the history of mankind we deal in cycles or with progress.

It is true that the Egyptian civilization, after the glory of the pyramid-building Pharaohs had passed away, gave way to slow decline. Babylon and Nineveh rose to glamorous heights only to fall and decay. The glory of the Hellenes and the Romans is but a memory today. After the promise of spring, the fruition of summer, and the harvest of autumn, they all, it seems, had to face the deadly chill of the winter. The Indians and the Chinese also had their great days but after having reached a certain level, they failed to progress. They were living in a state of fossilization when the Christian West "opened" them by force.

The civilizations of the ancient nations seem to have been destroyed. The culture of contemporary non-Christian nations seems to have been arrested and fossilized. However, this is not the whole story. This is true only when we consider them apart from the whole and not as dependent and integral parts of the entire human race.

Is it not natural that progress on the national, racial, and regional level should be limited? Is it not natural that on this level it should even come to an end? The nations, races, and regions are only tributaries to the great flow of human civilization. Although they add their part to the whole, they are only carrying a portion of the entire effort.

However, the transitoriness of the particular does not negate the permanency of the whole. The fall of the individual does not necessarily imply the end of the group. The decline of the particular civilizations does not preclude the progress of the whole human race.

The bygone civilizations of history are said not to offer any hope, as they move aimlessly toward their final destruction. However, their existence was purposeful. They partook in the common struggle for the general advance of the whole human race.

Besides rejecting the belief that the seeming end of the regional civilizations justifies the denial of general progress, we refuse to accept the thesis that the existence of the regional civilizations was purposeless and that their fall was final. What happened to them was not a full and complete ending. Their achievements are not lost. They did not disappear without leaving any trace of their existence. A historic civilization is not an organism. One cannot apply, for instance, the life pattern of an individual human being to the composite unit of which we speak when we talk about a civilization. It is picturesque, but deceiving, to draw imaginative comparisons, as Spengler did between periods of the civilizations and the four seasons. Moreover, to base scientific speculations on artificial parallels is misleading.

Ancient regional civilizations might have fallen, but they did not disappear altogether. Babylon, Athens, Rome are not dead. Their greatness lives in our own achievements. What they accomplished did not perish. Our own civilization is the best vindication of their immortal glory. Their achievements are part of our civilization as our accomplishments will enrich the culture of future generations.

Although the pre-Christian and non-Christian civilizations, after they had lost their vitality, showed signs of decomposition or fossilization, the ability of pre-Christian and non-Christian men to progress remained unaffected by these temporary local defeats. Men only waited for the very last of the great regional civilizations, which seems to be ours, to come to their rescue and to provide the necessary stimulus to make them move forward again. In terms of the millennia of human history, the period of their stagnation, due to the exhaustion of their own spiritual forces, was not long. It is about coming to an end.

No particular civilization perished completely. Such civilizations have either been absorbed by our vital Western civilization and thus have helped to build the future of all humanity (as was the case with the different Mediterranean civilizations) or they have been temporarily checked awaiting regeneration by some new stimulus. The revitalization is provided by the impact of the Christian civilization which carries in it the promise of salvation for all. The stalled civilizations have waited for rejuvenation so that they could be united in a universal civilization to come.

66

All the particular civilizations have had a mission to accomplish. They have swelled the tide of the ever-broadening river of universal human progress. All particular civilizations have contributed to the same great end: the ennoblement and final spiritualization of the human race according to the will of its Creator.

As far as the problem of progress itself is concerned, we should not be disheartened if it seems hard for us to observe it. The natural feeling of frustration resulting from relapses and reverses in man's historic march should not overcome us. True enough, progress is not steady; it is far from continuous. Great efforts seem to have been made, to no avail. Great achievements seem to have been lost. Moral lessons, acquired by painful processes, seem to have been discarded. However, in spite of the defeat of particular civilizations the common battle for human progress has gone on. The war, fought for the sake of all humanity, has never been lost and it never will be lost. The dark forces of faithlessness, ignorance, backwardness, and human discord have fought back hard, but they have been continuously and steadily pushed aside by the forces of progress. Recorded history is too short to allow us to appreciate sufficiently the progress that has been made on the whole front. At the front of general human advance there are and there always have been weak points. Sometimes the state of human affairs is indeed very gloomy. But in general, in the distance the contour of a promising future has become more and more discernible.

Man, because of his creaturely limitations will never be able to comprehend eternity. While space, as far as our globe is concerned, is understandable in human terms, man never will be able to understand time. Time leads to eternity and eternity is divine. The human mind cannot seize its significance. But progress is measured in time. That is why we have difficulty in sensing it.

However, the fact that progress is not steady and is hard to observe does not mean that it does not exist. Man has no reason to despair. Nothing is lost. We might zig-zag, but in the long run we zig-zag forward. If we look at the whole instead of the particular, we have no reason to be discouraged. The main stream of general human civilization is steadily broadening. The waters of the national and regional civilizations are swelling it. The ocean is in sight, the ocean of a common human destiny, the ocean of human co-operation, the ocean of universal civilization.

If we believe in one human race, we cannot but affirm the existence of progress and the general forward march of mankind. Taking humanity as a whole and not as some have artificially separated it into compartments of regional civilizations, one cannot discover any sign of autumn or winter. No sign of growing old can be discerned. We have no reason to despair and wait for the inevitable, the predicted end. In a later chapter we will detail the stages of man's progress.

4. DOOM FOR THE WEST OR SURVIVAL?

The proponents of the cyclical theory, having accepted the general pattern of separate regional civilizations characterized by predetermined life-spans and inevitable destruction, are eager to apply this pattern of gloom to our Western civilization. According to what they imply, ours also is a self-motivated civilization, having an organism-like independent life. They apply the same rules to Western civilization as they do to all the foregoing great regional civilizations. They state that our civilization has well passed the zenith of its achievement and has spent all its youthful energies. According to the cyclical theorists, we are traveling in the late autumn of our existence as a separate culture and are facing the chills of the cruel winter with final destruction and decomposition coming.

What can one say at the sight of this dismal picture as it has been painted by Spengler? Above everything else, it is false because, as we have said, it is completely unrealistic and unwarranted to depict history in terms of regional units and regional civilizations. History is not a simple anthology of the stories of the individual regional civilizations, as it is not the aggregation of the individual national civilizations, an idea rejected by the Spenglerians themselves.

The Spenglerian conclusion about the fall of the West, based on the premise of the absolute disappearance of the individual civilizations, is also false because, as previously stated, what seems to be the downfall of the particular civilizations is not necessarily an unretrievable end, if we consider it from the point of view of the universal civilization to come.

However let us accept—for argument's sake—the Spenglerian premises that, first, civilizations are the ultimate units of human history and, second, that these regional civilizations perished or are about to perish. Let us assume that human history expresses itself in regional civilizations. Let us suppose that the preceding regional civilizations ignominiously perished and disappeared into nothingness. Would this mean that our own civilization has inevitably to follow in their footsteps? Would this mean that Western civilization has to disappear? Do we not have anything more than they had? Do we not possess something which would enable our civilization to survive?

It is only human to think of oneself in terms of exception. We recognize that what is to follow seems to endow our civilization with some special mark of distinction. However, the task of demonstrating our special standing is undertaken not to glorify our own civilization but to support our belief that neither we nor the human race are necessarily facing decline, fall, and decay. Let us proceed, therefore, to show that our own Western civilization has something more than the preceding civilizations had.

We have to show that our civilization has a chance of survival, though the preceding ones are said to have perished, because it is different from them. Therefore, we have to find out in what respects our civilization differs from foregoing regional civilizations. We must also ask ourselves whether the points of difference, if any, are great and important enough to qualify our civilization for survival?

Before we enumerate the points of difference between our civilization and the foregoing ones, we want to stress with special emphasis the importance of one of the reasons for the better chance of our civilization to survive. There is one supreme comfort which we have and they did not have. There exists one all-outstanding and all-important difference between our civilization and all the foregoing and co-existing civilizations: *Christianity.* They did not have the divine promise of salvation—a promise which indeed was not given for our earthly salvation's sake, but which makes all the difference as far as the survival of Western civilization is concerned, and, indeed, of all human civilization.

The differences on which our hopes are anchored are:

1. The basis of all the differences between our time and theirs—as we have just stated—lies in Christianity. While we may not have applied Christianity as we should have to the solution of our temporal problems, it still has opened to us the road toward real progress in the highest sense of the word.

2. Pre-Christian and non-Christian civilizations did not have democracy. Now, thanks to Christianity, we are marching on the road toward an ever more progressive democracy, which, in turn, can be considered the temporal base of our material progress. Although we may not yet have realized perfect democracy, we are conscious of its essence and of its paramount importance.

3. Thanks to democracy, we have built modern technology. The pre-Christian and non-Christian nations never dominated and never used the forces of nature in the measure in which we are using them today.

4. Thanks to modern technology, the material foundation of a global political unity is laid. The means of communication and transportation render the building of a global state probable and make its control distinctly possible. The so-called "world empires" of the past never were global in the proper sense of the word. They stayed regional, since the lack of proper inter-continental communication and transportation precluded the building and the control of global political units.

5. There are signs in our day that, due to Christianity and also due to the physical contact brought about by technology and the budding idea of international democracy, the feeling of universal brotherhood is stirring in the hearts and minds of man. The idea of world community is germinating. None of the pre-Christian civilizations and non-Christian civilizations had unselfishly and consciously nourished sentiments of universalism. Their empire builders were motivated only by the ambition for conquest and exploitation, not by the brotherly feeling of co-operation and consideration of the interests of all the peoples of the earth.

In these points of difference our hopes for survival are anchored. These are the reasons why we are not fearful of the future. They encourage us to believe that the great human adventure is not foredoomed to failure.

In the following chapter we shall take these points of difference under examination, so that we can fully understand the hopes we entertain for the survival of our civilization and for continuing human progress.

CHAPTER III

CHRISTIANITY, DEMOCRACY, AND TECHNOLOGY

1. *HOPE FOR SURVIVAL: CHRISTIANITY*

Our chief reason for believing that our civilization will not perish is Christianity. It makes all the difference in the world.

Why do we think that Christianity will preserve us from degeneration? Did not the other religions give the spiritual energy necessary to keep their respective civilizations going? Did they not fulfil their mission? We recognized the desire of man, irrespective of color or race, to solve the problem of the unknown and his craving to find the reason for his own existence. All the religions represented this elementary aspiration of man. Christianity did not create the problem. Christianity solved it.

It is also true that all the great regional civilizations were based on some great religious belief. Man could only build civilization, he could only progress in the material sense if his spiritual problems were, or at least seemed to be, solved. Man could only progress when his peace of mind was assured by faith in a higher order, inspired by divine power. All the great religions well understood this crucial need of man. Their original inspirations were of an altruistic nature.

Neither can we say, as much as we believe in the revelatory nature of Christianity, that it arose without preparation and without any connection with other religions. The "fullness of time" was the result of a gradual historic process. It represented a state of spiritual refinement which came about progressively.

Why is it that while we recognize all the merits of the other great religions, we still think that Christianity is the only religion able to show the way toward progress? It is because we believe that Christianity is the crowning of all of the religious aspirations of man. We do believe that unlimited progress was made possible with the revelation of Christianity.

What makes Christianity outstanding among all religions? What makes us believe that, with Christianity to guide him, man will not perish? What makes us think that Christianity opened the way for progress? The reasons are as follows:

1. Christianity is universal. Unlike Judaism, to which we owe so much, Christianity has a promise for all the people of the world. Christianity does not close itself within the confines of one country. It does not stop at the border of a nation or at the limits of a region. It can solve, and it is solving, the problems of the whole human race. It spurs man toward international progress. It is a truly international and universal religion. It will help mankind to make the next step toward fuller integration on the political level.

2. Christianity does not give any concession to the selfish interests of the individual or the group. It does not give in to the pressure of the egoistic impulses of man. Unlike Mohammedanism, it is not the religion of one privileged sex. It does not condone practices based on egoistic motivation. Vicious usages can not find justification in a society based on Christian principles. Disgraceful practices, inspired by individual or class interests, have no place in a Christian community. Egoistic motives, when institutionalized, sap the vitality of any organization and consequent degeneration is bound to set in sooner or later. This was the case with all pre-Christian or non-Christian civilizations.

Progress is the result of common effort exerted by all the members of a community. The consideration of the interests of all the fellow-members is the secret of co-operation, and co-operation is the way of progress. *Christianity promotes progress, as it teaches self-denial and love and patience towards others.* These are the ingredients of co-operation.

3. Christianity has not only an interest in the spiritual salvation of all men, it is also sincerely interested in the earthly life of man. It does concern itself with the happiness of man in this world. It does want to bring its message to

all who live on the face of this earth, while they live in this world. Christianity offers the truth to all men and with the truth it makes them happy here on earth. Christianity definitely has an interest in this world. It is not indifferent to the earthly action of man. Unlike Hinduism and Buddhism, it does not preach retirement. It calls for human effort to perfect ourselves while living in this world.

4. However, Christianity above all is a promise for a better life beyond this worldly one. Christianity, besides being the recognition of the universal brotherhood, signifies something much higher; it presents the most noble faith in the fatherhood of God. While it is concerned with human behavior, while it teaches the brotherhood of man, it is above all a religion. Unlike Confucianism, it is not a moral code. Therefore, it is capable not only of directing man's steps in the field of earthly action, but also of standing beside man in the hours of trial, as it represents the divine promise of a better world beyond our human imagination. It consoles man, when earthly consolation is of no avail. In this imperfect world of ours, it supports man with the joyful assurance of the perfectness of God the Father. It enables man to reach the heights of complete spiritual elevation. It also assures a peaceful balance of mind, and thus enables man to wrestle with the hard problems of the world. With this spiritual uncertainty eliminated, man is better equipped to carry the heavy burden of this world. Man is fearless if he is a Christian.

5. Christianity is pure and simple. It does not offer hiding places for superstition and sinful practices. It sheds light on the unknown and discourages obscurantism. It does not stand in the way of progress, as did so many other corrupted religions. It opens the way to progress.

6. Its regenerative nature is beyond doubt and is amply proven by history. While its outward structure, in its different institutionalized forms, is often beset with the dangers of degeneration and fossilization, it has always succeeded in purifying the individual churches which professedly accepted it. Such was the strength of its divine inspiration that sooner or later it has succeeded in restoring its churches to their original purity. The Reformation is the best proof of the

point. Also in our day we again and again find groups motivated by Christian inspiration working with the vitality of the days of the revelation. It is also of capital importance that the regenerative force of Christianity has kept the secular institutions of the Christian world from degeneration and decay. This divine vitality has kept Christian mankind on the straight road and often restored half-forgotten values. While man never could elevate himself to the heights of its teaching, Christianity has been strong enough to guard Western civilization from being arrested or destroyed.

7. The most important reason for our optimism is the radiant example of the divine Son as revealed in the Scriptures. So-called historic documents are missing. Secular records of His utterances are not available. The supreme simplicity of the holy records, the unparalleled style of the apostles, inspired by their faith and sincerity, is the best testimony to their veracity.

Christ's life is the most shining example of completely spiritualized earthly life. The unattainability of His example is the best proof, if proof is needed, of His divine nature. Nothing within the reach of our imagination could have influenced man's fate and changed the course of human history more for the better than did the sublime example of the God-man.

He did not only bring salvation to man's soul. He did not only open the portals of heaven to man. He did not only bring escape from other-worldly retribution. If adhered to, Christianity also promises escape from the inferno of this life—and this life can be an inferno, if we give free, uncontrolled play to the inducements of the flesh and to the egoistic inclinations of our materialistic nature. Man never could have overcome the impediments of his original sin of destructive selfishness without the sacred example of his Savior. We could have found no escape from the dark fate of dying civilizations, no hope of progress, without the glory of His inspiration to love each other. In the light of this truly courageous interpretation of history, who could doubt that the social inspiration of His life, translated into human co-operation within ever-growing and broadening groupings of men, has paved the way towards our more advanced society and in it, towards all modern achievements?

The nightmare of ever-recurring deadlocks, innate in all civilizations built on material selfishness and particularism, was dispelled by Him who gave His life that man should live in peace of soul. By Him were we saved from disaster through discord and division, who was the living example of the ideals of love for his fellow-man, of human co-operation, and of self-sacrifice. Henceforth, inspired by His self-effacement, a just society, built on Christian principles of human equality, became possible. It is due to Him, the proclaimer of the idea of universal brotherhood, that new horizons toward a world community are even now opening up. With His appearance, the fear of man's destruction by deadly egoism was dispelled and the way toward progress through communal and international co-operation opened. A new world is about to dawn because He lived.

The greatest and most important difference between our age and the pre-Christian epoch, between our civilization and all non-Christian civilizations, lies in the fact that we have Christianity and they did not have it. The rest of the differences are all subordinated to this all-important and paramount fact. They are all related and can be traced back to Christianity. Let us now take a look at them.

2. THE POLITICAL APPLICATION OF
CHRISTIANITY: DEMOCRACY *

Interestingly enough, the typical modern scholar, with his heavy bias against "dragging religion into scientific research," does not see any connection between democracy and Christianity. He must accept the fact that democracy, as we know it, developed in the Christian West, but since he rules out any providential view of history, he can offer no explanation of the phenomenon and may, indeed, go so far as to classify the correlation as one of those interesting coincidences, interesting to note but not particularly significant.

But was it only coincidental that democracy as we know it developed within a specifically Christian context? Is the relationship between the Christian faith and the democratic system purely casual? Or is the relationship, in some respect at least, a cause-and-effect relationship?

It is certainly poor scholarship to eliminate, without further examination, the possibility that there is a close relationship between Christianity and democracy and that, at least to some extent, this relationship is one of cause-and-effect. One of the advantages of working within a Christian frame-of-reference is that one need not restrict his range of vision as sharply as must the doctrinaire secularist who keeps brushing against the divine mantle but dares not admit that it exists.

So—what does history have to say?

It may be assumed that men in all times and in all places have displayed fundamental similarities and have enjoyed equal potentialities for development. Pre-Christian men and nations had, indeed, embarked upon the road toward de-

---

* This part appeared originally as an article in the January, 1953, issue of *The Cresset* and is reprinted with the permission of the Valparaiso University Press.

mocracy and had built civilizations which still fill our hearts and minds with awe. The Sumerians, as an example, had great respect for law, and their laws restricted the powers of the mighty. The Athenians developed a kind of democracy which still, deservedly, merits our admiration. The Chinese, very early in their history, restricted inherited political rights, and, during two millennia of Confucian society, maintained a remarkable degree of social mobility.

But the more one studies history, the more one feels the tragic failure of pre-Christian and non-Christian civilizations to achieve what we understand by democracy. The more one marvels at their high technical civilizations and the products of their hands and minds, the more one is struck by their dismal failure to recognize the equality of all human beings in their political orders. At the very heights of what we to-day consider their magnificent achievements, barbarous and sinful practices and hideous social abuses were casting their dark shadows over their technical accomplishments and even over the great products of their minds. Thus it might be said that these civilizations, from the very start, were carrying within them the seeds of decay and disintegration.

The people of Athens had developed a remarkably high type of democracy and may well have been the first to recognize democracy as a political system. But the advantages of the system were confined to a limited body of citizens who inherited their status. Foreigners residing in Athens passed on their inferior social status to their children. And, to darken the picture still more, the whole Athenian economy was based upon the exploitation of a slave class which had essentially no political rights.

Among other peoples the story is similar. The Jews differentiate between themselves and the Gentiles, and discriminate against them. Moslems differentiate politically and socially between men and women and generally assign an inferior position to women. Hinduism, despite all the noble inspiration of its thinkers, finds its social expression in a rigid caste system and in a dehumanization of women. Buddhism, though it expresses man's highest aspirations for spiritual purification and perfection, has historically been associated with an almost unlimited exploitation of the masses by vested hereditary interests.

78

In spite of all their high inspirations and aspirations, none of the non-Christian religions stood explicitly for absolute human equality and the brotherhood of all men. And so, as time went on, discriminatory practices developed and were condoned or even supported by these religions. They adapted their teachings to the necessities of existing political and social situations and adjusted their dogmas to oblige the rich and powerful. What remained of supernatural and mystic higher inspiration was twisted to suit the interest of a ruler, a class, a sex, or a race. Some of these religions even developed hideous rituals, such as human sacrifice and suttee, which were not finally abolished until a few decades ago. And it is significant that the abolition of these practices coincides with the acceptance in these lands of Christian influence, if not of the Christian religion.

In contrast to all of these, the implication of the divinely inspired Christian principles of human equality and the brotherhood of all men is completely clear. Their meanings are unmistakable. The very essence of Christianity is the fatherhood of God and the brotherhood of all human beings without even the shadow of discrimination of any kind. While the primary concern of Christianity is not of this terrestrial world, the earthly implication of its command to love our neighbors as ourselves is clear. It does not permit any discrimination between men and it does not condone privileges of any kind for anybody. In a human sense, Christianity is all democratic and only democratic. The inspiration of Christianity to realize pure and complete democracy is unequivocal and indisputable. In a Christian society, in a Christian state worthy of the name, no political, social, or economic discrimination can be permitted. Moreover, the high inspiration of Christian universal brotherhood is the best hope of humankind to build international democracy in a better world of institutionalized world co-operation.

Certainly Christianity did not come to give democracy to the world. But it was inevitable that in a world inspired by Christianity democracy should develop. Democracy is clearly implied, even postulated, by Christianity. It was not incidental that before the coming of Christianity none of the non-Christian civilizations produced what we understand today as "democracy," even if the very word "democracy" dates back to pre-Christian times.

And so, although we certainly do not deny that democracy in a limited sense existed before Christianity, we do say that it took the insight of Christianity to bring democracy to fruition. Nor do we say that Christianity brought democracy into the world overnight or that the democracy that we know today is complete and real. Like Christianity, democracy is constantly in the process of becoming.

The road that led parts of the Western world to their present relatively advanced stage of democracy was long, devious, and hard. After Christ's ascension from this earth and after the democratic communities of the first Christians had disappeared, the dark shadow of the pagan past all but extinguished the early light. In the Middle Ages, despite the shining influence of exceptional personalities, the danger of decay was ever present and ever menacing to the institutionalized segment of the Christian church and, with it, to the European community. For a while the democratic implications of Christianity were all but forgotten, and it appeared that the Christian church might head down the same road of idolatry, superstition, and social injustice which had befallen other religions. With real Christianity pushed aside, its political inspirations had no chance to germinate. Social and economic injustice were rampant, and even the church shared in their perpetration.

One of the most illuminating of the proofs that Christianity and democratic practices are closely related is the fact that the real beginning of modern democracy dates back to the time of the Reformation. It was during this time that Christianity was restored to its real meaning and the church purified from pagan usages. As the light of the Reformation was turned on the basic Scriptures of Christianity, its democratic inspirations became evident. Protestantism is democratic because it is Christian. With the Reformation, a slow, gradual process of political democratization set in. The more emphasis a particular Protestant group put on the Bible, the more democratic became its inspiration. The role of the so-called "lunatic fringes" of the Reformation is indeed great in the political process of democratization. The "non-conformist conscience" was as religious as it was political.

If the democratic progress was slow and gradual, the teaching of the diverse Protestant churches implied from the very beginning (sometimes contrary to their own statements, dictated by expediency) complete democracy, embracing all elements of the population. The example of the "levellers" and the "diggers" to this effect should be clear enough. It was also quite logical that from the time of the early reformers who translated the Bible into the language of their respective people and made it available to the people at large, the exploited peasants tried to apply the equalitarian principles of Christianity to their own depressed situation and revolted against the oppressive rule of their landlords.

Under the inspiration of revived Christianity the slow and unconscious drive to build political democracy began. However, it took long centuries before the masses of the West began to profit from the changing situation brought about by applying Christian principles to politics. In this gradual process of democratization the Protestant Churches, especially the non-conformist churches of England, played a paramount role. No less is it true that wherever the Protestant churches, forgetting their pure Christian inspiration, joined their cause with that of the ruling classes or dynasty, the progress of democratization was slowed down, though by no means arrested. Neither is it to be doubted that the Church of Rome was revitalized in all respects as it was touched by the challenging effect of the Reformation. The terrible danger of fossilization and decay was lifted. New and progressive forces asserted themselves in the ancient structure of this church itself. It again became Christian. If it did not help immediately to open the way to political democratization, it made a special and not unsuccessful effort to regain and keep the attachment of its masses. At the beginning of democratic fermentation, in Roman Catholic countries such as France, the forces of progress attacked the church, as the latter allied herself with the absolute monarchy and the feudal classes upholding it. Only after the general acceptance of the principle of popular sovereignty did the Roman Catholic church raise her voice for the rights of the masses and in defense of their economic interests.

What is important in this respect is that, while competition with the so-called leftist forces for the souls of the masses and for their support gradually forced all Christian churches into accepting a more and more democratic stand, the standard bearers of democratic and social rights from the very beginning were those religious movements which had no other worldly consideration than to disseminate the message of Christ concerning the brotherhood of all men and the fatherhood of God. They were never allied to any vested interests, nor did they ever become the satellites of any worldly power. They were of pure Christian inspiration.

The fact that democracy found seeming support from anti-Christian forces—such as some óf the rationalist supporters of the great French Revolution, the worshippers of reason, the Marxist socialists, and the atheists of humanitarian tendencies—does not prove much. They might have denied the revelation of Christianity, as indeed they did, but they could not help but be influenced by its teachings as they lived in a world of Christian tradition. The very atmosphere of the modern epoch was, and still is, saturated with Christian thought, in spite of the fact that pure and real Christian faith was, for a long time, and still is, definitely on the decline. Neither does the fact that many past and present non-Christian leaders stand for the very highest ideals prove more. Their inspiration and their stand for democratic ideals did not and does not come from non-Christian sources. Though Gandhi's India was not a Christian country, he himself came and stayed in the closest contact with Christianity and absorbed its teachings to the fullest measure. He lived in a community which was part of a Christian empire. If non-Christian and non-Western nations apply democratic principles and build seemingly democratic states in our days, they do it because in our times the whole world is slowly accepting Western political standards. These standards might not in all cases be of Christian inspiration, but they are nevertheless the products of a world of Christian tradition.

82

However, it should not be forgotten that the anti-Christian forces which brought or pretended to foster democratic thoughts and action, such as Marxism, more often than not did considerable harm to the cause of democratic progress. Such was the case with Marxist bolshevism. As the bolsheviks based their calculations on materialism, they generated eruptive and destructive forces which inflicted deep wounds on humanity, tore up the world, and caused destructive revolutions, without furthering the cause of human brotherhood and equality. What is worse, they have no use for political democracy, for in their deterministic philosophy no place is left for the self determination of the individual on which this form of government is based. Political democracy is inevitably discarded or the fight for it is given up as soon as the bolsheviks seize power.

In the light of what was said before, we can assuredly state that it was under the predominant influence of the forces evoked by rejuvenated and refreshed Christianity that democracy won its first battles in the West. In England, this process of democratization worked through the gradual extension of voting rights to ever greater masses. The old forms were kept, but in the framework of ancient traditions the essence gradually became more and more democratic. The non-conformist churches were in the forefront of the fight. They were the actual strongholds of the democratization process. Their reward was the continuous loyalty of the masses. The influence of Marx on the British labor movement was and is negligible. On the continent of Europe, the building of political democracy was a more belated, bloody, and resisted process. This was partly due to the fact that the state-supported and corrupted churches, forgetting about Christian principles, did not stand on the side of those who fought for the economic interests of the masses. At times some of them even supported the suppressors of the people and the vested interests allied to them. Their unchristian attitude cost them the attachment of tens of millions of their adherents. It swelled the growing number of godless and faithless Europeans who were lured into the camps of the various false prophets. Whatever the stand of the official churches in Europe, the influence of Christianity on the democratization of the West in general remained paramount.

It is logical that as soon as the oppressed are conscious of their collective desire to shake off the burden of slavery and exploitation, they first will aim at the attainment of political rights. The recognition comes early to them that political participation in the direction of the organized community is the most important weapon to gain improved economic and social status. The underprivileged classes of our modern time cannot help but see that those who monopolized political rights before the rise of the principle of popular sovereignty were only too apt to misuse their political power in order to secure for themselves economic and social advantages. In the course of history, politically privileged classes have always known how to gain special social standing and how to monopolize the wealth of their country for themselves.

In the democratization process of the modern West, the recognition of the importance of political rights came at a relatively early stage. As we have seen, political and social groups related to and inspired by certain Protestant sects of Britain unhesitatingly proclaimed the principle of complete equality of all men as implied by Christianity and clamored for equal political rights for all classes. The standard symbolizing the political equality was picked up by the bourgeois class in the great French Revolution and in the American Revolutionary War. The movement to establish political democracy, stirred up by the emotional and intellectual stimulus of these events, slowly engulfed all the Christian West. Gradually it became all-embracing, fully conscious of its importance, organized and world-wide. The great stimulus came after the modern labor class, born in the wake of the industrial revolution, embraced the cause of political democracy as its own. This class soon recognized that its best chance to gain all around equality lay in the gradual extension of the voting right. The fight for universal suffrage began. Establishment of political democracy was thought to be possible by gradual evolutionary methods. As early successes were gained by employing democratic methods, the labor class of the Western world dropped the revolutionary pretenses and became one of the most important factors in building democracy by democratic means.

Finally the effort of generations was crowned with success. After the first World War, the process of the gradual extension of political rights terminated in the introduction of universal adult suffrage. Thus political democracy became a fact in the Christian West.

While the building of political democracy went on, in connection with this process and with the help of the gradually extended political rights, the economic conditions of the masses were slowly improved and social differences minimized. However, vested interests were only gradually relinquished. The dragons of economic and social privilege were not to be killed with one blow. Although the fight for political rights finally was won and the relatively advanced type of political democracy was built in the West, much still remained to be done as far as social and economic justice was concerned. Even in the Western states, now based on political democracy, much social and economic injustice exists. The inspirations of Christianity are not all considered and carried out in human relations. What proved to be even more fatal for the world as a whole is the fact that only few Christian countries established political democracy, while the overwhelming part of the world never enjoyed its advantages.

The incompleteness of democracy in the West and the complete absence of it in the East made it possible that, at about the same time that the long struggle for political rights came to a successful end in the West, non-Christian forces could successfully challenge political democracy. This challenge came from the forces which emphasized social justice and equal distribution of wealth. They promised to build social and economic democracy. However, they did not believe in the political participation of the masses in the direction of their destiny. Although their first success came in the East, where no political democracy existed, their ideology was the most logical product of the secularized Western spirit. They based their theories on the unchristian materialism of the nineteenth century. Marxism is not Eastern. It is Western. It does not represent a new philosophical departure. It is not revolutionary in this sense. Marx can only be understood in terms of Hegel.

What is important about Marxism for our purpose is that Marxism does not believe in political democracy which, inspired by Christianity, presupposes man's freedom of determination and emphasizes the importance of the individual. Like the materialistic bourgeois philosophy on which it is based, Marxism believes in inexplicable material forces innate in things which drive the world on its predetermined course of destiny and which shape the future, uninfluenced by man and uninspired by God. In its denial of moral justice based on individual responsibility, it is bound to play down the importance of the individual in politics and thus to reject political democracy.

However, while Marxism is eliminating political democracy, it does give the false hope of a more just social and economic order to many parts of the world. This is one reason for its appeal to the masses of the East. Having never known the advantages of political democracy, they know all too well the misery of hunger and the shame of inferior social status. And so, promises of social and economic democracy are temptations hard to resist. Marxism even has an appeal for people in some Western countries where political democracy has been achieved but where economic oligarchy and social aristocracy have perpetuated low standards of living. And even those nations which enjoy the most refined type of democracy are not, by reason of lingering social and economic injustices, immune to the danger of bolshevism.

If bolshevism is the inevitable product of Western materialism, and if it thrives best under conditions of economic and social injustice, so does fascism. Fascism, though it grows from a common root with bolshevism, poses as the alternative to bolshevism. The pose has attracted many who forgot or never knew that both these authoritarian systems derive from a rejection of basic Christian doctrines concerning man. Both grow out of the Western world's

86

imperfect understanding and practice of Christianity. Bolshevism and fascism, equally mortal enemies of political democracy, will never be overcome unless we eliminate the cause of their rise, which is our unchristian behavior in human relations.

To succeed, we have only to follow the teachings of Christianity: to believe in the fatherhood of God and to try to build the brotherhood of man in this world. If we are consistent in applying all the relevant implications of Christianity to our political, social, and economic practices, we will not have to fear either bolshevism or fascism. After building political democracy, we should eliminate the vestiges of social discrimination and we should bring about economic conditions everywhere which would assure at least a minimum living standard to all and eliminate economic exploitation from the face of the earth.

However, there would be one more hurdle to overcome. Bolshevism, when it arose, besides promising social and economic democracy to the exploited and debased people, also held out the hope of a better world for all the nations. Its promise of a better life was given to all humanity without any discrimination of race or nationality. It fully realized the rising interdependence of a world society. It fully recognized that no solution is possible anymore on the sole base of a national state. But does Christianity not imply co-operation among all nations? Can democracy be confined, if Christian, to the limit of a nation?

Democracy is not Christian if it recognizes human rights only for one's fellow-countryman. How could democracy stop at the border of a country? If we recognize all men as our brethren, how can we love only those who talk the same language and hate those who, by some historic accident, live on the other side of the national boundary line? Democracy, like Christianity, must be all-inclusive if it wants to be successful. All the misfortunes and tragedies we have heaped upon ourselves, especially during the last centuries of secularized thought, are in great part due to the fact that we did not apply the implications of Christian brotherhood to our political action. Where we failed most signally was in the increasingly more important field of international relations. Ever greater and ever more destructive wars have resulted from our failure to live up to one of the most important commands of Christianity: to love our neighbors as we love ourselves.

From now on, even those happy and fortunate nations which attained a relatively high degree of political democracy and (thanks to fortunate circumstances) could afford a certain measure of isolation and forget about the misery-ridden and war-torn part of the world will have to share the fate of the less fortunate nations. Democracy is no longer possible in separate national states. It has to be universal if it is to survive. The dangers of the surrounding world are so immense that no country can afford the luxury of democracy unless the rest of the globe shares in its advantages. As the peace and the war had to come to be recognized as indivisible, so will democracy have to be considered, from now on, as indivisible, no more the privilege of a few nations. The world cannot stay half-free and half-slave. National democracy is an idea of the past. International democracy is the only democracy possible in our time of complete international interdependence.

Earlier civilizations did not have democracy in our sense of the word. It took a long time until the political implications of Christianity were understood. The West first established political democracy. That is not enough. We have to keep on working to eliminate the remnants of social discrimination and, if possible, we have to get rid of all vain and unnecessary distinction among men and nations. We also have to win our battle against misery and privation; we have to improve living conditions everywhere in the world. This is the only way to eliminate dissatisfaction from the mind of the masses. If we succeed in doing this, we will be able to overcome the two-fold danger of bolshevism and fascism. But this is not all. We have to create a world safe to live in. Peace will reign only if we succeed in building international democracy.

Modern democracy is the product of the Christian era. It did not flourish in pre-Christian times and in non-Christian countries. Although it is less important than Christianity, it is absolutely vital in modern society. At this stage of human development, it is the only political way by which man can solve the problem of government without the hazard of ultimate anarchy and destruction. While at this juncture of history democracy is badly in need of internationalization, under Christian inspiration it could solve the problem of institutionalized international co-operation. It is one of mankind's hopes to save its advanced heritage and to survive.

3. THE PRODUCT OF DEMOCRACY: TECHNOLOGY

There are two outstanding factors which we who study the relationship between Christianity, democracy, and technology have to consider at this point. First, modern technology developed in democratic countries. Second, as democracy grew and thrived so did technology. The connection between democracy and technology is not just co-incidental. The two are linked in a relationship of cause and effect. This is just as true as it is true that it is not accidental that democracy developed in Christian lands.

Democracy aims at freedom, just as lack of democracy leads to slavery and the subordination of the many to the few. Democracy offers freedom to the individual and assures freedom of his activities. Democracy brought about freedom of research and raised the intellectual standard of the masses. Freedom of research started technology on its way. Modern technology has its roots in the epoch of the rejuvenation of Christianity when, thanks to the Reformation, democracy also set out on its way of development. This is not surprising at all, since true Christianity is the denial of all forms of slavery, including that of ignorance. The individual is a slave if he is ignorant, the slave of those who know. Christianity is the liberation of the individual from all oppression. It liberated man also from the darkness of superstition and ignorance.

As we have seen under point two of this chapter, the germination of modern democracy can be traced to the Reformation. At the end of the eighteenth century, in connection with the French Revolution, democracy was ready to move again. Along with slowly extending political rights, ever broader masses were given the possibility of learning and education. Education ceased to be the privilege of the few. In the growing cities, the best ground for the development of modern democracy, the interest of the people in public affairs and participation in politics grew. With

90

growing interest and participation in politics, the need and possibility for better and broader education grew accordingly. With gradually improving standards of learning and with increasing numbers of learned people, modern technology was about to start on its phenomenal career. The growing number of people who contributed to technological work is explained by the democratic trend of education. Important discoveries brought about by this trend opened the way for laying the foundation of a technological age.

Democracy, and with it learning, made new strides during the nineteenth century. Technology followed in its path. The face of the Western world began to change. Railroads and highways were built, metropolitan cities sprang up, industrial plants mushroomed all over the Western world.

Progress in technology and resulting industrialization increased the need for working hands and thus the population of the Western countries began to grow by leaps and bounds. Labor started to organize and clamored for more political rights and better material comfort. The proletariat became more and more vocal and demanded its share of the growing wealth achieved with its help. Political democracy was sought for in order to use it as a means to lifting the living standard of the masses.

With political rights gradually extended, the importance of the workers grew. During this process it became evident to those who were engaged in the fight for progress that no real political and economic equality was possible without equality in educational facilities. Neither could the dignity of man have much meaning unless equal educational possibilities existed for all. Due to the development of democratic thought, Western mankind relentlessly moved toward a momentous goal: free and compulsory education for all. Education was to embrace the children of all classes. Mass education became possibly one of the most important factors in modern industrial society. The important role that compulsory free education played in the rise of this technological age, and with it in the radical change of human life, is not fully appreciated.

This process of educational democratization, coupled with technological advance, was well on its way when the twentieth century dawned on the world. The masses became more and more conscious of their human rights. The feeling of subordination of the employed class gave way to the class-consciousness of the workers. They exchanged their former fatalistic acceptance of their hazardous and hard life for the firm determination to improve their lot, whatever the costs. Labor became engaged in class war.

However, with the gradual extension of political rights to cover growing numbers of manual laborers and with slowly-improving living standards, labor, without being too conscious of it, lost its revolutionary fervor. While the old slogans of revolutionary Marxism remained on their lips, the conviction grew in their minds that it was not only possible, but preferable, to use evolutionary as opposed to revolutionary methods for the attainment of their legitimate aims. Western European labor accepted parliamentary democracy as an instrument to attain a better life, and, after the second World War, in several Western European countries labor parties participated in or even controlled the governments of their respective countries.

Parallel to this process of democratization, ever-advancing technology completely changed the life of Western man. A new age was rising, an age of democracy and technology. New means of communication and transportation helped to open the farthest corners of the globe. It was not long before all regions of the world were linked in an economically interdependent unit. Western standards were gradually extended to all parts of the earth. A network of many thousands of miles of railroads, endless strips of superhighways, lanes of ever more luxurious and ever faster transoceanic liners, and rapidly multiplying fleets of airplanes flying at never imagined speeds, linked the globe ever closer, thus creating an interdependent global society.

The relationship between progressive democracy and broadening education was mutually stimulating in this age. On the one hand, progressive democrats fought for compulsory free education; on the other, the raising of the educational standard of the masses enabled them to claim political rights and a greater and greater part in government. This gradual process of political democratization, stimulated by extended educational facilities to ever more people, finally led, after the first World War, in most of the Western countries to the introduction of universal adult suffrage. It is hard to stress sufficiently the importance of this step. It was truly an epochal achievement. Mankind, politically speaking, came of age. Due to universal adult suffrage, indirectly based on Christian principles, the political parties representing the industrial workers and the peasants began to play a role of paramount importance in the political life of their respective countries.

With political equality practically attained and with higher cultural standards, wage earners all over the West were becoming anxious to gain a higher living standard. They wished to share in the enjoyment of the comforts of modern life made possible by modern technology. Hard battles were fought for higher wages by labor, led by the labor unions. The gradually-rising wage-level had a salutary effect, not only on the income of the employees but on industry as a whole. Due to the higher spending-power of the wage earners, they could offer to buy not only necessities but some industrial articles which before were considered luxuries. Labor became one of the most important customers of industry.

Thanks to the great number of these new customers, the industrialization of the West was further stimulated. The expanding market, having gained many millions of new customers, made mass production profitable. Mass production, which can be considered a consequence of democratization, lowered considerably the price of industrial articles. This, in turn, raised by millions the number of customers, because the lower prices were within their reach. Factory production was increased again. As democracy marched ahead, the wheels of industry began to turn faster and faster. This spurred technology to new experimentation and natural sciences to new discoveries. With advancing democracy, technology progressed steadily.

It is not accidental that it was the leading democracy of the Western hemisphere which revolutionized factory production by introducing the assembly line method. The United States was not plagued by the impediments of feudal-

93

istic tradition. This gave an early start here to political democracy. Due to exceptionally favorable circumstances, the free people of this country were also the first to sense that political democracy alone is not enough. Man everywhere, besides being anxious to have equal political rights, is also desirous of attaining economic security, and if possible even a comfortable life. As a matter of fact, he is always tempted to use his political rights for improving his standard of life. In this country, more than anywhere else in the Western world, higher wages contributed—as stated before— to the bringing about of industrial mass production made possible by new technological methods. Mass production is democratic America's gift to mankind.

American industry used technology to serve the masses by serving its own interest. It lifted the living standard of the common man in order to make more profit. It can be said that, in general, capital and labor co-operated in this country. No political party was needed to fight for labor's cause, for the leaders of American industry understood the close connection between political democracy and technology.

While it is true—as explained above—that political democracy helped technology, it is also true that technology can pay back its debt by helping to bring about economic democracy. Today the working masses of the United States can afford all the comforts and luxuries produced by modern technology. Much has been done by American industry to secure economic democracy, this thanks to mass production, assemblyline methods, high wages, and low production costs.

On the other hand, it is not surprising that outside of the United States, where the close relationship between technology and democracy is not clearly understood and where there exists a big gap between the wealth of the rich and the poverty of the poor, labor is deeply involved in politics. Political parties, in general, represent the different social classes. The central problems of domestic politics are in general connected with the struggle between the social classes. Political democracy cannot work properly without a certain measure of social and economic democracy. France is a good case in point. With political democracy, but with an outmoded economic structure and a narrow-minded economic leadership, not willing to accept new production methods and reluctant to pay fair wages, France has much trouble on the political and social fronts. This explains the considerable strength of the French Communist Party, which has the support of the working class. The very political democracy is endangered if social discrimination exists and the living standard of the masses is low.

Based on democracy, technology brought much more than industrialization. Technological progress, the result of the great discoveries of our age, changed every aspect of human life and transformed the face of the earth. Through large-scale mechanization and scientific soil-conservation, agriculture was also transformed so that it has been able to provide food for the population of the world, which had multiplied during this epoch. Thus the ever-growing demand of industry for labor could also be satisfied. Due to ceaseless revolutionary development in communication and transportation, distances in terms of time have shrunk to insignificance. The word "sanitation" has become a meaningful one. Thanks to science, man has been able to check plagues which, before the rise of public sanitation, periodically hit mankind with devastating effect. The life expectancy of the individual human being has been lengthened beyond all expectation.

We have just seen how, in the West, technology developed under the stimulation of democracy, after democracy had evolved under the inspiration of Christianity. Let us now see what might explain the fact that the pre-Christian and non Christian civilizations never enjoyed democracy in the western sense of the word and never could create an advanced technology.

It is not surprising that we encounter different conditions of life in the pre-Christian and non-Christian countries from those which prevail in the West. Because democracy could not develop, since Christianity did not light its way, the non-Western countries were left not only in spiritual darkness but also in material backwardness. None of the pre-Christian and non-Christian nations succeeded in establishing democracy, since they did not have the spiritual inspiration of Christianity which postulates human equality. Not having succeeded in building democracy, they lacked the foundation necessary to bring about advanced technology and with it general material progress. Technology had no chance to develop because the prevailing atmosphere of political oppression was not conducive to the advancement of general education and the furtherance of free and umhampered research.

The state of affairs in the ancient lands clearly illustrates the fact that, without the acceptance of universal political rights and without the recognition of the supreme worth of the individual human being, the material prosperity of a country will stay limited to a very thin upper crust of the society. The situation prevailing in pre-Christian times also shows how greatly political oppression handicaps the unfolding of man's knowledge and how it blocks the advancement of his technical know-how.

Before the coming of the Christian era there never existed a strong trend toward general political equality, and therefore in the atmosphere of exploitation and arbitrary oppression only the interest of the ruler and the privileged few were considered. The ruler was not only the absolute political master of the land, he also was often worshipped as a god. All of his subjects were at his mercy. The idea of the supreme worth of the individual was unknown.

There was no lasting progress toward democracy (though attempts were repeatedly made) in pre-Christian and non-Christian lands; consequently, in spite of all the architectural glory of the ancient empires, the masses lived in abject poverty, for nobody even dreamed of using the prevailing technical knowledge for the improvement of their living conditions. There was no democratization, consequently people lived under the constant fear of starvation; for the ruler, not being responsible, often did not care whether his subjects had enough to eat or whether they starved. There was in general no concern to relieve the misery-ridden masses from their heavy burden and assure tolerable material living conditions for them. In the absence of political democracy nobody paid any attention to the needs of the people.

Learning itself was more often than not the privilege of

a caste and the masses were kept in ignorance. Often even the clergy conspired with the political elite to withhold the light of knowledge from the people. Thus political oppression went hand in hand with ignorance, and ignorance bred misery. That this is true is well illustrated by the few exceptions, such as Greece, where progress toward democracy opened the way in a limited sense toward the rise of sciences and material advancement. However, as a rule, science was cultivated on the basis of "art for art" and not many attempts were made to apply its principles to the raising of the general level of welfare.

In spite of the fact that ancient man excelled in the different fields of handicraft, no attempts were made to develop methods and devise equipment to multiply industrial production in order to supply the masses with what we today consider as elementary necessities. The prevailing handicraft industry amply served the interests of the privileged few. They were not interested in applied knowledge beyond the requirements of their own needs. Nor did they care about the improvement of the known technical processes, once they had their rich share of goods. Nobody dreamed about technology, for the rich did not need it.

We do not intend to minimize the very important material achievements of the ancient civilizations. The genius with which God endowed man always finds rewarding ways to express itself. Great things were accomplished in the fields of science and art. But in the absence of democracy, all the advancement was used in the interest of the few and served the glorification of the mighty. The interest of the masses was considered very little or not at all. The person of the subject was abused, humiliated and enchained. The people did not profit from the technical "know how" of ancient times.

After a prodigious rise, accompanied by momentous material achievement, the ancient civilizations were bound to level off and decline. They were not built on the firm foundation of Christianity and democracy. They did not stand for their own people. Spellbound but saddened, we look at the faded glory of the works of art built by the ancestors of misery-ridden peasants and shepherds of today.

The descendants of empire building nations would not even have a recollection of the glory which their country once was, were it not for Western scholars who have succeeded in reconstructing in imagination the ancient past. The ancient people themselves, after the decline and fall of their civilization, lost even the techniques of how to build monuments of great artistic inspiration. Could the Cambodians reproduce the ancient architectural beauties of Angkor Wat or the Egyptians duplicate the glory of the pyramids of Gizeh?

Before the inhabitants of Asia and Africa came into contact with the Christian West, they did not know about modern technology. After the vitality of their respective civilizations was spent, and until the white man appeared on the scene, they lived a rather stagnant life. The West found them under conditions which were very much like those which prevailed among them a thousand years ago. Their ways to clothe themselves, to shelter themselves, and to work had remained unchanged through centuries. Their tools and appliances were like the ones employed by their ancestors far back. Their rivers remained unregulated through the centuries, their roads remained few and primitive. Their natural resources, though potentially very significant, were not even tapped. The soil was left to the hazards of erosion. Sanitation was non-existent. Plagues were an ever present danger. Floods remained a periodically recurring menace which yearly took the lives of thousands. Famine was taken for granted. Man did not stand up against nature to defend himself and fight back. It was an abject life for the poor. Man was subordinated to the whims of nature, which reigned almost uncontrolled. But the principal enemy of man was man himself. The privileged few steadily abused and constantly abased the destitute many.

The situation did not change much until our own days when the non-Christian part of the world became more and more exposed to the influence of the West. Not that the West lived up to Christianity's inspiration in its relation to the East: the annals of Western colonialism are not filled with golden pages of Christian achievements. Long after the opening of the East, and in spite of the presence of the white man, living conditions remained very much as they were before his coming. However, under the impact of Western civilization (but not necessarily intended by the European masters) a gradual change for the better was brought about. In our own day, the people of the East and of the tropical lands have embarked, on their own initiative, on the great adventure of westernizing their countries. They aim at the improvement of their very low standards of living with the help of Western technology, for which they have the highest respect. They are not so very sure that democracy can offer much to them. They show even less interest in Christianity.

The fate of the less-developed part of the world is indeed one of the most important and most burning problems of mankind today. The peace of the world is connected with it. Technology certainly can play a role in the solution of this question.

As we have seen, democracy helped technology to develop in the West. In its turn technology is helping in establishing more general domestic well-being in the Western countries. It also could help the Asian and African nations to get rid of their present poverty. The resulting more equitable distribution of wealth among the nations would help to eliminate or at least lessen the dangers which menace mankind today. It would help to bring about international democracy. The appalling misery which afflicts the greater part of humanity is causing much unrest and contributes to the dangers by which modern mankind is beset today. Technology is at the service of man. It could help to eliminate poverty from the earth. If all nations would pool their forces in a common effort, conditions could be brought about under which the wellbeing of the Western nations could be made more secure, and at the same time a better life could be assured to the misery-ridden hundreds of millions of Asia and Africa.

Modern technology was given to mankind in order to help man go forward on his march towards progress. It was developed in a time when it was most needed, when the world was beset with fears that emanated from the Malthusian theory. In a time when the warning was sounded that the

99

earth would not be able to feed the rapidly multiplying human race, technology brought the promise of a better and more prosperous world.

However, in spite of the importance of technology for modern man we never should forget that it is but the final product of a process which led mankind from Christianity to democracy and finally brought about technology itself. It is hard to imagine, indeed, that democracy could have developed in any other but a Christian context. It is also difficult to think that modern technology could have been brought about without Christian democracy. Nor should we forget that material well-being and high living standards do not assure the happiness of the individual human being. Man needs freedom and he also needs faith. Well-being cannot survive long if human freedom is attacked and eliminated, just as freedom cannot survive the elimination of the Christian faith.

Our age is justly called the age of technology. The pre-democratic, pre-Christian era had nothing like it. The importance of technology in modern life is paramount. Modern man's economic well-being is the result of technology. Our living standard depends on it. It also offers man the possibility to institutionalize the existing global interdependence and to solve the problems of permanent peace.

4. TECHNOLOGY AS THE BASE
OF WORLD ORGANIZATION

Besides the fact that we have Christianity, democracy, and technology there are other differences between our civilization and the preceding ones, between our age and the foregoing ones.

One of them is the fact that due to the high development in the technological field there is a distinct possibility of building, running and controlling a territorially limitless political community covering the whole world. Technology created the means of global communication and global transportation. The resulting global intercommunication has made the rise of a world economy possible. Global intercommunication, along with inter-mingling of the different races, also made the spread of Western civilization possible so as to gradually engulf the world. However, political unification of the world is slow to come. This in spite of the fact that the technological foundation of a world-commonwealth is laid. Let us review briefly the means which would render possible the organization, administration, and control of such a world-commonwealth.

Western man has penetrated all the corners of the world and has opened them for intercommunication. Globe-girdling travel on land, water, and in the air has become possible. One can fly around the globe in a matter of days. Transportation of goods and their exchange in limitless quantities has become relatively easy and cheap. The living word is transmitted from the farthest corners of the world and heard at its destination practically in the moment it is uttered. Pictures taken at far distances from the United States appear in American newspapers the next day. Television is also destined to girdle the world in the near future.

It is easier and less time-consuming to reach far away corners of the globe today than it was, not too long ago, to reach neighboring countries or even neighboring townships.

Due to the tremendous strides made in the development of fast air-communication, the problem is not how to reach the next continent and how to make travel between continents faster. The problem is, rather, how to deliver the air-passenger faster and safer from the airport to his final destination, be it his residence or his place of business. Time is lost not by spanning continents, but by overcoming city or suburban traffic jams.

The human race is still divided into national entities. But there are clear indications that the trend is inevitably toward regional and, at a later stage, toward eventual global unification, as this becomes more and more possible through the same means which brought an end to the self-sufficient economies of the nations and which are causing the withering away of the national and regional cultures.

Technology opened the world for the European imperialistic nations. During the nineteenth century such nations as Great Britain and France amassed colonies all over the world and established what are referred to as world empires. The means of global communication and transportation—these achievements of a technological age—made their empire building possible. The Asian and African victims could not resist. They lay prostrate before the superior technology of the European imperialistic powers. However, the colonial empires were not world empires in the true sense for they did not cover the whole world. They only linked territories situated on different continents. Only in this restricted sense could, for instance, the British empire be called a world empire.

The first world war was only in name a world war. The actual battle ground was confined to, and the important battles were fought in, Europe. No arms of global character were used during its course, with the exception of the different classes of war-vessels whose ranges easily covered the oceans of the globe. However, the first world war had global ramifications, not only because Japan was indirectly involved, not only because the Near East figured prominently in the chronicles of that war, but rather because man sensed that technology had such potentials in the field of armament that it might enable a nation with imperialistic inclinations to become a deadly menace to all other nations wherever they happened to be located. The entrance of the United States into the first world war could be explained by such apprehension. Germany might not have entertained plans of world domination, as the war propagandists of the allied nations declared. Should she, however, have succeeded in triumphing over her European enemies, she might have embarked with the help of her outstanding technical knowledge on some adventure aiming at the establishment of a world empire.

During the first world war the natural scientists and the researchers of applied technology did their best to develop new weapons for the use of their respective fighting forces. Great strides were made in the course of the four years of the war. Old weapons were perfected and new ones devised. Machine guns became more and more important in the fighting. The range of the mechanized heavy artillery was progressively extended. The newly invented tanks contributed substantially to the final victory of the Allies. However, as far as the future was concerned, the fact that the airplane was also employed in actual combat was of paramount importance. The war plane was destined to become one of the most important of the global weapons.

Thus technology induced some great European powers to embark on building colonial empires. It lured the Germany of the Kaiser to try her luck with empire building even at the risk of starting a world war. However, no conscious intention of world conquest can be imputed to the European imperialistic nations. The awareness of the desirability of a world state and the conscious promotion of such an aim is clearly seen in the case of the Bolshevik empire. The Marxist scheme is global in ambition. It is not an accident that an ideology which is so much concerned with industrial relations should develop the first grandiose plan of real world unification. Marx, in a time when industrialization and technology were in a relatively infant stage, devised a doctrine which was conceived in terms of an age which was to dawn a full century later and which was going to be dominated by the fear of global weapons.

With complete awareness of the Bolshevik plan of world domination, and inspired by the same respect for technology and industrialization as the Bolsheviks themselves, Hitler, overestimating Germany's power, unleashed the second world war and plunged the world into the greatest cataclysm of man's history. The second world war is justly called global. All of the great powers of the world participated in it. It was not fought predominantly with infantry battalions. The main weapon of this war was not the rifle any more. During its course technology outdid itself in creating weapons which gradually were to change military operations into what is called "Push-Button Warfare." Besides the war-vessel, the war-plane played a dominant role in the fighting. The airplane industry produced models of heavy bombers whose flying range enabled them to reach into the center of any great European country from any of their neighbor's territory. Airborne operations were tried and perfected; they contributed substantially to the winning of decisive battles. Amphibious landings played a most important part in bringing Germany, and especially Japan, to her knees. Germany in the closing stages of the war surprised the world by sending self-propelled missiles onto the cities of the British homeland. Here was a weapon which was destined to become one of the most important among all presently known arms of potential global range. But, as it is well known, the self-propelled rocket was not the only surprise at the final stage of the second world war. A greater surprise was yet to come. The atomic bomb was dropped on Hiroshima and contributed to the swift ending of the Pacific war. If considered along with the ever growing radius of the long range bombers which can bridge the oceans, and if refueled can span the globe, the atomic bomb can justly be called a really global weapon of the most murderous effect. Thus with the splitting of the atom, natural science has crowned all of the services which it has rendered to Mars.

Even before the introduction of the two weapons of potential global character the military strategists had to resign themselves to the necessity of some very hard rethinking of some long accepted strategic axioms and to the advisability of taking decisions aiming at the early scrapping of many ot their favorite theorems. The second world war without any doubt clearly showed that there would be no safe place in a coming war. It also proved that there would be no territories which could be considered impenetrable to an invader. The idea of impregnable defenses had to go too. Distance lost its prime importance in war. Some old military legends, such as the one about the impenetrability of Russia's wide back spaces, had to be relegated to limbo. With modern ways of war-communications and supported by global weapons of all types, the armed forces of a great power can blast their way anywhere. They can penetrate any corner of the world in full force. They can defeat an enemy, whatever the size and the extent of his territory. Natural barricades do not exist any more. "Defense in depth" lost its prohibitive meaning. No individual, no nation can find a hiding place anymore in case of an atomic war.

Our planet can be conquered in its totality by properly equipped armed forces. To have better armed forces than the enemy offers the only protection. The best way to acquire better armed forces is to keep ahead in technological knowledge and in the development of industrial capacity.

The greatest and most important lesson to be deduced from the military history of the second world war is this: The globe can be unified and organized by force. The means to do it are at man's disposal. Technology is producing them. In our times of power politics, world unification in the form of organized world government could come through world conquest.

But could such a forcibly conquered world-empire stay a going concern for any length of time? Is the vastness of the global territory not prohibitive to the successful running of a world state? Once established, could the world empire be properly administered and controlled? If we have any illusions in this respect, let us look at the forcibly established and arbitrarily ruled Soviet Union. This huge territory, the greatest of all existing sovereign territorial units, which covers about one-sixth of the land surface of the world, is very much a going concern. It was born in one of the most frightful revolutions the world ever knew. A devastating civil war was fought on its territory for years. Invading forces sapped its energies. It was again sorely tried in the second World War. All these misfortunes seemingly did not undermine its vitality and its capacity to survive.

The Soviet state was built to carry out an experiment which involved the complete reconstruction of the old economic, social, and political structure of the country. Total spiritual and material re-education of the population had to be undertaken for the success of the experiment. Old spiritual values were given up overnight. The ancient religion of the people was scrapped. Property relations, as they existed before the Bolshevik regime took over, were junked and new ones substituted. Never in man's history has an experiment aiming at the realization of a theory involved such profound changes in the life of the people and never were changes made on such a huge scale. The individual was not considered in this revolution. His interests were ignored, and his person abused. During the twenty-six years of Stalin's dictatorship this empire was ruled by a man who after his death was described by his own successors and former henchmen as mad. Still the empire survived. It is still accepted by its own people, seemingly without any open resistance. It is also accepted by the world at large, the rest of the nations apparently having no other choice than to put up with this power.

The Soviet Union has much trouble with its people. The terror used against them in the course of rebuilding the economic and social structure is proof enough that things were from time to time extremely difficult for both the rulers and the people. Still the leaders kept complete command over their domain as they controlled all the means of communication and transportation and were able to profit from those advantages, which the possession of modern armament gives to all governments in the suppression of rebellions. Even the Nazis, during the short duration of their domination over Europe, had the conquered territories under control and could suppress any open resistance with relative ease in spite of the fact that simultaneously a terrific war was absorbing most of their military force and engaging by far the greater part of their fire power. Had they won the war, with all the weapons at their disposal, their control over the conquered land could have been made absolute.

If the Soviet empire, with its formidable size and with its racial complexity of unusual magnitude, involved as it is in economic, social, and political experimentation, can be administered and controlled successfully, why could not an empire extending over the whole globe, once established by force, survive and be ruled from one center in our age of technology? It would have even a better chance to survive, because, unlike Russia, it would not be encircled by enemies.

The global means of communication, and the weapons which can help a power to take over the world, can be used both to organize a world empire and administer it from one center and to suppress any revolt of the subjected people. Telephone and radio could bring, in a matter of minutes, all needed information from all the far-flung parts of the empire to the center. Directions could go out through the same means and reach the organs of local administration in minutes. In case of revolt, well paid and favored armed forces, stationed at strategic places, could be rushed by air, or transported rapidly by motor vehicles, to the place of trouble and could nip any uprising in the bud.

It is, then, possible to conquer the world and also to administer and control it for the sake of a self-centered empire, built around an ambitious nation by a power-crazy leader. If this is so, why would it not be possible to organize by cooperation the population of the world into a political community? The same means of communication and transportation, which have made the globe into an economic unit and which are now in the process of linking culturally the whole human race can be used also to establish a co-operative world-commonwealth without the use of force. The same means could be used to administer, to direct, and to control such an organization in peace.

It is true that on the road of historic progress man has been more apt to heed force than to consult his intelligence. Could we not hope, however, that with all the warnings of the past and all the advantages of the present, this time he will avoid tragic mistakes and costly false solutions? Inspired by Christianity and enlightened by his intelligence he could build by peaceful cooperation of all nations the needed world commonwealth.

Today we have the technical means of world organization. What about the pre-Christian era? How far were they from such a goal?

Technology as a means for world organization is the gift of the West; a gift of doubtful value though it may be. The pre-Christian man had nothing like modern technology to help him build anything bigger than a regional empire. Means of communication and transportation were primitive for the purpose of carrying out even such a modest job. The range of weapons was infinitesimally narrower than it is today. It will be well to remember that even the Western man until the closing period of the Middle Ages depended on pre-firearm types of weapons for defense. The great historic European battles of this time were fought with bows and arrows. It is hard to believe that in a not too removed age Englishmen and Frenchmen fought and killed each other with fast flying arrows just as the Indian Five Nations fought and killed each other. Once the firearm was introduced, Europe gained a great military advantage over all other continents. However, the next step in arms technics took several centuries to come. Even part of our own Civil War was fought with the muzzle loader. The real revolution in military technics set in with the first World War.

In spite of the primitive weapons, attempts at uniting and dominating greater regions were made in all epochs. It even came to the establishment of so-called "world empires." They, to be sure, only covered regions. In the case of the Alexandrian and the Roman empires we refer to the territories conquered by these empires more modestly as the "known world," though even this is too pretentious, because by now we know that both the Macedonians and the Romans naturally never thought that they had reached the end of the earth. They knew about the lands beyond their empires.

The rise of ancient regional empires could be explained by different circumstances. The simultaneous temporary weakening of neighboring nations was one of them. New military strategy, such as used by the Roman Legions, surprising the potential victims, was another. The nomad empire-builders, such as the Golden Horde of Genghis Khan, had the advantage of great mobility, made possible by their horses. Their military strategy, based on their equestrian ways, confused and overwhelmed the sedentary European farmers and merchants.

Technics played, until very recently, a relatively subordinate role in war and in conquering of territories. Man power and draft-animal made up not only the means of war-transport but the actual combat forces. The individual warrior was the main element in the battle which led to conquest and empire building. Victories were gained and were accounted for in terms of man's personal courage, force, and prowess, not in terms of fire-power and technology.

The administration and control of the ancient empires likewise rested on the same primitive means of transportation. Control was exercised by military force primarily made up of man-power and the hauling capacity of the draft-animal. Roman control over their far-flung empire was made possible by a system of manually built roads, all converging on Rome, the center of the realm and the seat of its military power. However, the Roman chariots and other vehicles were drawn by horses. Thus, there was a direct connection between the endurance of the draft animals and the territorial extent of the empire. The speed of the horse limited the radius of the Roman power. The Mongols controlled their subject peoples, dispersed all over the vast territories of Eurasia, by spreading terror through their fast riding warriors, who reached the places of troubles with relative ease.

In short, both the ways of conquest and the ways of control of the non-modern nations were too primitive to organize a real world empire. Had technology not developed into what it is today, regions never would have been connected by the means of global communication and transportation. Had technology not succeeded in devising all the dismal weapons of global character, we should not be living in an age when we can justly fear that an ambitious empire will take over the globe or a false ideology organize the human race for aims of doubtful value. As a matter of fact, without technology there would be no necessity to think of world organization, because we would need to deal only in national or regional economic units and because the regional cultures still would keep well apart.

As it is, however, technology, besides creating the many media of global communications and transportation which directly account for the rising of world economics and the fusing of world cultural standards and which offers the possibility of world unification, has devised also weapons which could be used to unite the human race by force.

The need and the technical possibility of linking the whole population of the world into one political unit are already upon us. The job undoubtedly will be tried. It will also be successful. But who will do it and how? Will it be done for good or for bad?

5. DAWNING OF WORLD-CONSCIOUSNESS

The fifth difference between our days and all prior ages is the slowly-developing awareness in the last generation that only by building a world community could we solve our common human problems. At this time this awareness is affecting the masses. It is not confined to dreamers and intellectual "crack-pots."

Mankind gradually is becoming conscious of the fact of its unity. It is becoming aware of the economic inter-dependence of all the regions of the world. It is awakening to the inevitability of further territorial integration. It is awakening to the necessity of the establishment of some working global political organization. This is not a consciously accepted conviction of the majority, from where no back-sliding would be possible. The feeling of human unity is not strong even in the minds of those who tend to accept it. The difficulty of entertaining ideas not backed up by human institutions and not supported by conventions is preventing many from adopting it. The fear of being ostracized by fellow-citizens for not conforming to the present political pattern of behavior based on the absolute sovereignty of the nation-state is a great deterrent to its spreading. The dread of the alien, the revultion against fusing into the same community with members of races of different colors who may not share our values, our moral standards, our customs and traditions, are terrible deterrents. In spite of all these, millions are affected by the idea of human unity and other millions are ready to embrace it.

Some people understand, others sense that something must be wrong with the political situation of the world. Total-itarian wars, world depressions, and world-wide social un-rests remind man that the crisis is global. All the underfed, underclad, badly sheltered, and war-weary masses are ready to accept the promise of a better life. They think in terms of economic salvation. But they sense clearly enough that material salvation has to be brought about by changing man's prevailing patterns in international relations. The brotherhood of man is for them, the brotherhood of all the hundreds of millions whose chief problem is how to hold body and soul together and how to keep their children from starvation. This feeling of unity within the underprivileged majority of mankind is made conscious in them by false prophets who are exploiting the present tragic state of affairs in the world. One of the reasons for the easy success of these false prophets is the fact that they appeal to the rising feeling of human unity and recognize the interdependent interests of men all over the world.

Here is the best proof that, deep in their hearts, people everywhere are becoming aware of the fact that the crucial problems of the time are not local, national or even regional in character, but that they are of global scope and can be solved only by the co-operation of all nations.

The importance of the rise of the feeling of human community cannot be over estimated. No world state can be built without it. If it is tried, it will not endure unless all human beings are linked by the common feeling of being members of the same human race and unless they believe in the idea of living together in one political organization. The conviction that "united we stand and divided we fall" applies to a world organization also and must become generally accepted before we can have any chance actually to erect one.

While the feeling of world community is budding in our time, this was not the case prior to very recent generations. Let us now take a look at the picture of the past, which we will better understand, if we start with analyzing how this feeling rises in man.

The feeling of human community comes from the belief in the oneness of the human race. If we are convinced that all men are alike because they are members of the same natural unit, we will feel drawn toward them and we will develop a feeling of community with those to whom we think we are related. In short the feeling of brotherhood will rise in us in spite of the existence of individual races, because in the light of the basic likeness of the members of the human races we will be able to overlook the insignificant differences between the differently colored groups. Once we feel that we are all members of the same natural community, composed of fundamentally similar human beings, we will be willing to join without fear in an organized political community for the solution of our common problems. This, of course, means also the acceptance of a constituted political authority with power to decide all disputes which might arise from the differences between the differently colored members. (This presupposes a certain uniformity of cultural standards, a question with which we will deal in chapter three under point two).

On the other hand, if man does not clearly realize the oneness of the human race and if he believes in the existence of fundamentally separated races, he will never fully embrace the feeling of community with all men regardless of race or color. Not having the feeling of universal community, he will not trust the members of the different races. He will dread them and will tend to underestimate their spiritual and moral stature. He will impute to them moral standards lower than his own. He will even attribute to them sinister vices. Not feeling any sense of community with them, he will not want to join with them in the same political organization. His distrust of them and his fear of them will keep him from recognizing a common political authority entrusted with the adjudication of conflicts. He will accept aliens into political coexistence only on his own terms. He will demand the subordination of the alien to the "racially superior" dominating group.

During the short course of recorded history man in general has had this negative attitude toward the alien. He has not embraced the feeling of community with outsiders. The alien has been dreaded and mistrusted. He has not been considered a member of the same human family. If he resided abroad, he shared no rights. His status was low and he was loathed. When captured in war, he was killed or enslaved. Even the cultured Greeks looked down on all non-Greeks and called them Barbarians. The Jews, in spite of their high religious inspirations, considered themselves set apart from the other nations, distinguished even by God as the chosen people.

Thus in the ancient times, man did not believe in the oneness of the human race. He did not have any feeling of community with the members of alien people. No feeling of universalism existed except in very vague form in the writings of a few thinkers.

Only with the coming of Christianity did the idea of human brotherhood find acceptance in man's mind. Through Christianity the spiritual base of universalism was revealed. It took the Christian world a long time to realize the full meaning of the command to love the neighbors as oneself. The Christian man of the Middle Ages struggled hard to live up to it in practice. Finally he limited its applications to the Christian world, though not even here did he meet with complete success. Whereas he was more or less successful in uniting the Western Christian nations for a while in a Christian spiritual community, his several attempts to form a corresponding political organization went on the rocks. In short, the man of the Middle Ages did not comply in practice with Christianity's command to consider and treat every human being as a brother, although his high aspirations in this respect cannot be denied. For instance the legality of war was questioned all through the Middle Ages and the recurrent problem of the just war was heatedly debated among scholars of the epoch. (This was a far cry from what was to follow in the modern epoch, during which International Law put the stamp of legality on war.) In books published in the time of the discoveries of the faraway lands, the "heathens" were considered as human brothers. European Christian jurists, such as the Spanish jurist-theologian F. de Vitoria argued on Christian principles for the natural rights of the natives.

It is not an accident that with the de-Christianization of Western man's life and thought, even what was before considered as the Christian European community became divided into warring nations, whose members ceased to consider each other as brothers. Members of different Christian nations became *alien* to each other in the most sinister sense of this word. This feeling of alien-ness grew to the point that killing the subjects of other nations brought honor to the individual.

Because the feeling of common human destiny was generally absent in the past, no chance for the building or survival of a global commonwealth could have existed, even if contemporary techniques had permitted the creation of such a state. People, as a rule, thought about their respective political organizations in terms of ultimate political realities and missed all feeling of universal community.

It is true that so-called "world-empires" rose from time to time. However, they were of short duration and they had nothing to do with universalism. They were formed by nations which, by extending their power beyond their original boundaries, wanted to glorify and enrich themselves. Their purpose was exploitation of the subjected people. No feeling of common destiny existed among the different groups which made up these "world" empires. They were not supported by that devoted attachment of their whole population which stems from the feeling of belonging to the same community. Sooner or later they were bound to fall because they were dominated by force and not supported by the community of emotions and interests.

In our own days, in contrast with the past, the feeling of common human destiny is beginning to grow. The budding feeling of universal human community no doubt stems from Christian inspiration, since faith in the divine creation of man posits the unity of the human race and since belief in the brotherhood of all men is one of the most important tenets of the Christian religion. Christianity is the spiritual foundation of the rising awareness of the common fate of men. While this is the basic truth, it is also true that the awakening of mankind to the fact of its unity can be directly related to the fact that an inter-communicating world exists with economic interdependence a crucial factor and with cultural fusion between the different civilizations in full progress. Man is beginning to sense the decisive importance for his fate of the great changes that were brought about in the course of the past few centuries. The gradual realization that he lives in an interdependent world is awakening in him the feeling of common human destiny.

Man is beginning to sense also that the promise innate in the global progress is great and that he is standing before the gate of a truly promising future. He is beginning to feel that the gate can only be opened by the united effort of all men. He is beginning to sense that the goal of human reintegration can be reached only by the will and the action of all.

But he must also realize, and he is beginning to realize, the dangers involved in a radically changed world situation. He must also be able to read the foreboding writing on the wall. He must realize the immensity of the catastrophe which might overtake him if he does not take the global step imposed by the fundamental transformation of human life.

The changes that transformed the world impose grave obligations and hard decisions on man if he wants to enjoy a bright future and avoid the final catastrophe. Although the rising awareness of a common destiny could help man to carry out the task of world organization, in its early stages it is endangered by the old human handicaps of stupidity, inertia, and selfishness.

Man can take the next step on the road of integration, because now he has the means to build a universal political community. He has also been awakened to the necessity of taking the decisive step. But will he not again let things take their course under the influence of his materialistic disposition? The problem is this: how can the feeling of belonging to the same human race grow strong enough to overcome the handicaps innate in man's nature?

To overcome man's materialistic instincts and thus give a chance to the dawning feeling of common human destiny to lead man toward the final integration, spiritual inspiration is needed. Here, too, dangers arise, for false inspirations are offering false solutions. It will depend on the kind of inspiration which man chooses whether or not he will be able to attain the goal.

Only the sublimeness of Christian inspiration can help man to overcome all of his innate handicaps and to fight off the tempting false inspirations. Just as the Christian spirit was behind the awakening of the feeling of human community, so now that the strengthening of this feeling is needed, man can again depend on Christianity. Christianity can strengthen the feeling of human community in man. Christianity can lead man toward the final integration.

The greatest promise that the feeling of common human destiny will ripen into maturity inheres in Christianity. This promise is based on the fact that Christianity does not know any difference between nations and races. The spirit is well expressed by Saint Paul: "There is no difference between Jew and Greek: for the same Lord over all is rich unto all that call upon Him." This inspiration is bound to strengthen the now budding feeling of human community in man and this offers hope that an organized world community will at last arise.

CHAPTER IV

POSSIBILITY OF WORLD ORDER
AND DIFFICULTIES

In the introduction to part two we indicated that the chief aim of this book was to discuss the possibility of the establishment of an organized world community. We made it clear that before we could come to any conclusion, we would have to refute certain misconceptions which influence many people who doubt the possibility of the coming of an institutionalized world order. We thought that certain implications of the cyclical theory are representative of these misconceptions. We felt that they had to be repudiated in order to open the way to clearer understanding of the problem. We enumerated five implications of the cyclical theory as discouraging the belief in a better future.

In order to refresh our memory we list these implications here again:

1. The largest human collective units through which history reveals itself are the different civilizations.

2. The civilizations of the different regions of the world and of the different ages of history are organic units with a predetermined and innate life-span, fixed in a limited number of years. They live out their given and restricted possibilities uninfluenced by preceding or neighboring civilizations.

3. Since all civilizations inevitably come to an end, there is always a complete new start. Civilizations come and go in cycles. Progress does not exist.

4. Our civilization, like the others, is doomed to fall.

5. All of these premises naturally imply the impossibility of universal unification.

These are certainly not encouraging statements. If we do not accept the original unity of the human race, if we do not believe that its destiny is one and indivisible, how can we suppose that the presently severed parts of it will ultimately form an organized world community? If we are unable to see the historic interdependence of the regions and civilizations of the world, how can we imagine that finally all of the different regional currents of man's civilization will unite in a mighty stream of unity? If we think of man's history as nothing else than a pure mathematical summation of the individual regional civilizations, with their organism-like lives of limited duration, how can we believe that there is a never-ceasing general forward march in history leading to unification? Finally, how can we believe in the mission of our civilization to accomplish its task if we make up our minds in advance that there is no difference at all between the present state of affairs and the world situation prior to the coming of Christianity, democracy, and modern technology.

The seriousness of these implications of the Spenglerian theory, casting dark shadows on man's future, induced us to take up the work of repudiating the implications in question. Let us see now how far we have succeeded in carrying out our assignment?

In chapter two, under point one, two, and three, we denied the first three of the Spenglerian implications. Under point four of the same chapter we listed the five differences between our own and the foregoing civilizations, which in themselves could enable the West to survive. All of chapter three was taken up with the detailed description of these five differences (our advantages) point by point.

We feel that we have succeeded in disproving the four implications of the cyclical theory. Summarizing what was said in the second and the third chapters, we repeat here that Spengler was wrong, because:

1. Mankind biologically is one indivisible unit.

2. Complete separation between the different geographical regions of the globe has never existed. The regional civilizations intercommunicated not only in time but also in space. That is, not only have the succeeding civilizations built on the heritage of the preceding ones, but co-existing,

geographically separated civilizations have also used each other's achievements.

3. Taking humankind as a whole, as it should be taken, we perceived a steady, though not always straightforward, movement in history. Considering the problem from the great perspective of the universal forward march of man from the hidden past into the unfathomable future, we have no reason to believe that there has been no progress.

4. We have the special advantage offered by Christianity, democracy, and technology and the dawning of world-consciousness, which themselves encourage us to believe in the survival of our civilization. The steady development of democracy, after Christianity had built a firm foundation for it, is a historic fact. So is the amazing progress of technology with the help of democracy. The awareness of a common fate is also awakening. Besides, we have no reason to despair over the future of our civilization, because we accept it as proved that even in the light of man's short recorded history general progress is discernible.

Thus, in the course of our discussion of the two preceding chapters, we have refuted the first four sinister implications of Spenglerian theory. We changed the negative implications of Spengler's theory into positive assertions. From the premises of a future doomed in advance we turned them into promises of a better future. However, the job is not finished. We still have to repudiate the fifth Spenglerian implication, that which postulates the impossibility of universal unification. This implication—as we will remember—logically followed the preceding ones and was derived from them. By refuting the four first implications of the Spenglarian theory we logically eliminated the fifth one also. However, as this book is written to prove the possibility of institutionalized world order, we want to discuss this problem at length and directly refute the fifth implication.

In the present chapter we will wrestle with this final implication of the cyclical theory. Our assignment would be only half carried out if we did not tackle this hardest job, the task of directly demonstrating the possibility of the coming of a sovereign world organization. While our four above enumerated assertions, which we derived from the reversal of the Spenglerian implications, encourage us in general to be optimistic about the ultimate future of international relations, we have to understand clearly why they make us actually hopeful. We have to reveal their immanent promise of providing a better life for all so that we shall be intellectually equipped to demonstrate the possibility of the rise of a peaceful and prosperous world.

Our aim is clear. As we did with the first four negative implications, we want to reverse the fifth Spenglerian negative implication into a positive assertion. We want to assert the possibility of the rise of a purposeful universal organization. We want to do this by taking our reversals of the first four Spenglerian implications one by one to show exactly why they encourage us to believe in a better human future. We will relate our four positive assertions to the problem of institutionalized world cooperation so as to prove the possibility of the latter.

In order to understand clearly our plan for this chapter, we enumerate here the gist of each of the four positive assertions on which we want to base our arguments about the reality of our hopes for a peaceful and better future.

1. There exists only one human race.

2. The different civilizations never lost contact with each other.

3. Viewed from the vantage point of universal civilization, definite progress is discernible in man's history.

4. At the present time we are qualified, both technically and intellectually, to build a unified world community.

In this chapter we will take up these four affirmations and one by one show why they encourage us to believe that gradually the world will develop into an organized political unit.

However, doing this we will not cover up the difficulties. We shall not be able to give clear-cut answers. We shall see that to build a better world is, to say the least, an arduous task. We shall face many problems which will have to be solved as we proceed. We shall encounter many difficulties which are obstructing the way. We shall have to point out the roadblocks. Can we expect a brighter future under such adverse circumstances? That is what we shall try to find out.

1. THE ONE HUMAN RACE IS BOUND TO ORGANIZE

In the second chapter under point one we proved that there is essentially only one human race. Christians and men of science agree on this point in spite of the visible physical difference between the so-called races. However, the existence of the differently colored human groups is a fact of great importance. A second crucial fact stands also out clear enough: the human race presently lives divided in many sovereign states.

Thus, men are partitioned by two different dividing lines: the one divides them into several color classifications and the other into many nation-states. Both divisions of the human race are of paramount importance. The past brought them about. The present is plagued by them. Man's future depends on whether he will be able to solve the crucial problem connected with this two-fold division.

The two-fold separation of mankind blurs man's vision to the essential unity of the human race. The separating colors are so apparent, the dividing nation-states are so self-asserting that man is bound to forget the ultimate reality of the oneness of the human race, and is tempted to become skeptical as to its implication concerning the possibility of institutionalized world cooperation.

This is the reason why we have to take up this problem here, because in spite of the fact of the oneness of the human race it would be hard to be optimistic about the coming of an organized world community unless we are able to appraise the importance of the fragmentation of the natural human unit. In order to understand that the ultimate reality is the whole human race, while the differently colored groups and nations are only transitory, it will be wise to see how the two-fold division evolved into what it is today. By relating the rise of the two-fold fundamental fragmentation, we will be able also to appreciate better the differences between them and to properly estimate their relative importance.

122

Let us see first how the color differences were brought about through history. As we know, once upon a time, all men lived together in their original home, the place of man's creation. However, due to overpopulation, a first migratory movement was bound to set in. This led migrating groups of the human race out of the common original fatherland into all corners of the globe. Separated from each other, living under widely diverse conditions, the individual human groups soon became exposed to various climatic factors and were altered by the effect of their different geographic environments. This brought a gradual though not substantial change in their physical appearance and caused some alterations of transitory character in their mental make-up, which accounts for the overemphasized but actually not significant particular racial characteristics. Thus, during the unaccountable millennia of unrecorded history, the so-called main races, characterized by different colors, were shaped into what they are today. It is well to remember that this process of race building never went on uninterrupted. Looking at it from the perspective of centuries, nature's process of differentiating races is a continuous one. It never comes to an end. Races are always in the process of becoming as they are biologically in relatively constant contact with each other. This transitoriness, resulting from the natural mutation of races, is a further proof that it is the whole human race which is the basic unit and not the so-called individual race. The whole human race is the immutable unit, created by God. It reflects the eternity of its creator; it is not subject to fundamental changes. The individual races, on the other hand, mirror the transitoriness of their physical surroundings. They reflect the changing nature of the factor which caused their variations: environment.

Thus, differences in "races" were brought about by the gradual effect of environmental influences. Here, therefore, we face changes visible on the person of the human individual himself, brought about by nature's processes, such as mutation in the color of the skin and the hair, in the shape of the skull, and so on. While the physical differences in the several colored groups do not affect the biological unity of the human race, their crucial importance for mankind would be hard to deny. Since the variations in the colored groups is the work of nature, these groups rightly can be called natural entities. On the other hand, the division of the human race into politically sovereign communities is the work of man and as such it is artificial. However, their effect on the contemporary international politics is even more important.

The story of the successive changes in man's political organization until the rise of the nation-state, into which mankind is politically divided today, is a different one. While nature was at work to partition the human family into groups by bringing insignificant, but visible changes to its members, man himself, probably soon after he became conscious of his existence, had to realize that personal safety and prosperity could only be had through human cooperation, and that cooperation could be assured only by recognizing organized political authority, vested with power of coercion. The story of the different types of political communities is a familiar one. The family and the clan, based on blood relationship, gradually gave way before organized political communities established by consent or imposed by the authority of a strong leader of outstanding ability. Man understood or was made to understand that the only alternative to a state of affairs where everybody fought against everybody was political organization.

Political organization has taken many forms in the course of known history. The tribal political organization fitted best the needs of the nomad, as it assured the necessary mobility to the members of the community, whose sustenance was derived from such mobile pursuits as hunting, fishing, and tending herds. Later, owing to the growing population-pressure, the time came when the hunter ran out of hunting grounds and the herdsman did not find new pastures. Men had to settle down to farming. A more sedentary political organization was needed: primitive kingdoms arose. City-states were mostly established by merchant and artisan communities. Both the nomads and the merchants tried their luck with organizing empires. Toward the end of this stage we see the rise of the modern national kingdoms which finally were succeeded by our own sovereign nation-states.

By this time well defined territories had been carved out by the politically organized national groups. They considered themselves self-directed and self-perpetuating ultimate entities. Thus, the human race became divided into the fenced-in units of independent states, which resented and tried to stop all intrusion from abroad. Inter-communication was made dependent on the formal permission of the political unit. In time of war, communication ceased altogether as in modern wars all the population became involved. Relationship between individuals belonging to different nations was determined by the character of the connection existing at the given time between their respective states. On the international scene, not individual human beings but political communities faced each other. This finally led to the principle of sovereignty in the most strictly conceived sense, which was to become the strongest theoretical weapon with which the self-aimed, self-perpetuating nation-states have vested themselves.

After this brief review of the origins of the two fundamental divisions, we wish to take up the work of evaluating their comparative importance. The two division lines, one separating the races and the other the political communities, never corresponded with each other. They cross and recross each other with bewildering irregularity. On the one hand the individual races live subdivided into many nation-states, on the other, states often count among their citizens members of different races.

It will be useful, for our purpose, to make here three special points to prove that presently, from the international political point of view, the division of the human race into nation-states is more significant than its division into individual "races."

First, while we have to figure only with the existence of four or five main individual races, we are obliged to deal with about ninety competing nation-states. The differentiation brought about by nature's work is therefore less complex than the one created by man, if for no other reason than for the numbers involved.

Secondly, in the case of the racial groups no confrontation exists between the individual and the color group of which he is a member. They cannot very well have opposing interests. This is because the racial units are not organized. They only happen to exist. They are the work of nature, not of man. No political authority governs them. They do not set up organs, nor do they decree laws. They do not impose obedience on the individual. He is not restricted in his original sphere of action by the racial group. He has no formal obligation to fulfil toward the whole. He is free to live out all his potentials as far as his relations to his race are concerned. This is just the opposite to the position of the individual as a citizen of the nation-state. As such his person is overshadowed by the power of the state and his interests have to be completely subordinated to the purposes of the state. "State interest" is an expression which if abused, can have the most sinister consequences for the human individual. The fact that the individual is so closely tied to the nation-state has important ramifications as far as the building of an international community is concerned.

Thirdly, the racial entity does not stand, at least not at present, in the way of organizing the world for general human purposes. The racial unit, not being institutionalized, represents no special interests. It has no organs, no leaders, no classes which would have vested interest in its survival. It cannot have a centrally directed propaganda machine to inculcate loyalty into the minds of its members. It has no schools to win over the hearts of the youth. It has no symbols and shibboleths. It has no anthem, no flag, no slogans, nor does it have red numbered days on the calendar to stir up emotions: hatred for those of different color and love for the race. In short, it does not hold the body and the soul of the members in slavery. The national state, on the other hand presents, indeed, a formidable obstacle on the road toward institutionalized world cooperation.

These three points show that in our day it is not the division of men on the color-line that is in the way of a purposeful world organization but the partition of the human race into nation-states. In this respect it does not make too much difference whether we face a nation-state with white or with black or yellow population. Presently, nation-states formed by non-white peoples are seemingly more inclined to support international organizations, such as the United Nations. This, probably, because they stand more in need of support. However, it is a question whether their newly found nationalism may not even more jealously watch over the sovereign rights of their liberated countries and oppose all limitations of sovereignty, even in the interest of a future world commonwealth.

In the present international situation, because of the cold war, the differences of color are de-emphasized. Along with nationalism, which is still very virulent, ideological differences are responsible for most of the international conflicts of our days. Both sides involved in the cold war do their best to win favor with the non-white nations. There are actually no international alignments based on racial affinity. (The Bandung conference of 1955 was not intended as such). For instance, both the Asian communist block and the Western-sponsored South East Asian Treaty Organization (SEATO) include nations of the white as well as of the non-white races. This state of affairs is not contradicted by the rising tide of anti-colonialism and nationalism in the Asian and African nations, which is one of the fundamental characteristics of international politics today. The prevailing ideological conflict, which divides the white nations, did much to help the colonial peoples to gain their independence.

Although not even international alliances are formed today on the base of racial affinity, the next step on the road of territorial integration might lead to the formation of racially controlled continental political units. We hasten to add that while this might become the case, it would by no means be a fortunate solution. However, fortunate or not, compared with the political division of the human race into the present nation-states, there are some obvious technical advantages of a state of affairs in which the color groupings would coincide with political units; this because the building of racially controlled continental empires would represent a more advanced stage in the historic process of territorial integration. First, the present number of ninety sovereign political communities would be reduced to four or five. This would eliminate much confusion resulting from the criss-crossing of such a considerable number of power-interests. Second, the average size of the sovereign territorial organizations would be enlarged, a fact which would give a better chance for the individual citizen to prosper. Third, since the main racial groups in general live in solid blocks, the number of persons living as members of minority-groups would be reduced. This, in turn, would cut down international conflicts resulting from minority disputes, a frequent cause of war today. Fourth, the geographic separation of the political units, based on continents, would be clear and distinct. The boundary lines would be unquestionable. They would be "natural". Territorial conflicts, which plague today's international politics and cause so many wars, would be reduced or even eliminated.

For these reasons political communities of continental size would be more congruent with the economic and cultural realities, as well as with the political necessities brought about by modern technology. They would correspond more closely with the advanced technological capacity of modern man than the nation-states do. They would be more viable from the economic point of view, if for no other reason than that they would dominate larger territories and unite more people.

Whereas this seems to be true, as a matter of fact, at this stage of technological advance and cultural fusion, when needs are global, it is already too late, even from the technical angle, to consider regional solution as desirable.

Should, however, the political division on racial lines ever come about, we would probably have a white commonwealth covering Europe with a narrow northern segment of Asia joining in, and North Africa possibly also included. (This in spite of the present ideological and religious differences). The larger part of Asia would form a populous yellow empire, while Africa south of the Sahara would be the Negro's domain. The Western Hemisphere would either join with white man's Europe, or else stay separate as a second white commonwealth.

In spite of the indicated apparent technical advantages of

a continental-racial solution of the problem of further integration, such a solution would have sinister implications.

Because the modern migration, mentioned in chapter two, has somewhat changed the clear geographic separation of the different races, none of the great continents, with the exception of Europe, is inhabited exclusively by any one race. Thus, regional and continental empires would inevitably include minorities of other races, though in their aggregate sum they would not come near the total of language-minorities living in nation-states today. This would cause trouble. The organization of the main races into hostile or competitive political communities would be also detrimental, in the highest measure, to the cause of the reintegration of the human race. It would bring new racial differentiations and would vent the flames of racial hatred, which easily could cause racial wars between the giant power-blocks with the danger of world destruction. In the atmosphere of racial hate even the idea of human brotherhood would be extinguished and this would end all great designs to erect a political fold for the human race. Empires based on racial entities could easily degenerate into international segregation with tragic consequences.

But inter-racial wars would not only endanger the idea of world unification. Since empires built on the base of racial entities would represent more viable units than the present nation-states, and since the visible differences between individual races would make the confrontation of the political units more clear, in all probability it would be even harder to induce these continental states to cede their sovereignties to a universal unit, as is today the case with the nation-states. If racial empires ever should be built, the present two separating lines would merge into one. It is true that there would be only one division between men and men, that brought about by racial differences, but the one line would be so much stronger. Nationalism, the love of one's country, would be considerably strengthened by the fusion with the sentiment of racial consciousness and loyalty. The separation into political units would be underlined and enforced by the fact that each racial empire would unite all members of a particular race. Political separation would be supported by racial separation. Nationalism would not only express the loyalty of the citizen to the political community; it would also reflect the feeling which comes from the consciousness of racial identity. Racial-nationalism, in a world in which racial-states would face each other, would be a formidable and terrible force.

It may seem far fetched today, when in international politics racial differences are played down, to talk about racial-empires. However, we can cite instances from the recent past to prove that racially inspired attempts to build regional empires are not unknown. Japan's much advertised war-time plan to establish a so-called Asian "Co-prosperity Sphere" was dangerously close to realization in the form of a racially dominated empire covering the greater part of Asia. Hitler openly boasted about his intention to take over Europe for what he called the Aryan race. He planned to establish, in fact he was already engaged in establishing, under Teutonic leadership an empire covering a territory which would have extended beyond Europe.

At this point we ask ourselves whether the new Negro-populated states of Africa, such as the Gold Coast and Nigeria, which are in the process of becoming independent, would not logically tend to unite in a great African commonwealth? Could they stand alone? Will they not want to establish a United States of Africa? As far as our own Western Hemisphere is concerned, can one not see a natural tendency in the United States, especially since the days of the so-called dollar-imperialism, to lead or at least to protect the whole continent and to organize it into a unit for the good of the white American? What happened to the North American Indian? What is happening to the Indians of Latin America? For that matter, can the United States afford for long to look passively at the economic misery of the masses, at the social injustices and at the never-ending political turmoils so characteristic of the countries south of its borders? Political, economic, and social conditions in the southern part of the Western Hemisphere are such that they invite communist penetration. In spite of all the revolutions going on, the real revolution is still to come in South America. Can the United

States patiently wait until such time? Will it not have to assert its leadership?

After having dealt with the problem of the two-fold division of the human race, let us now face the second question which we assigned to ourselves under this heading. This is the problem of how the nature and the needs of the individual are leading man toward the political unification of the whole human race.

God created the human individual as a member of the whole human race. Among all groups of which man may be a member, with the exception of the immediate family only the human race carries God's hand-mark. The rest of the groups are man-established or are brought about by nature's mutating influences. Considering this fact, it would be natural that the political community in which men live would be based on the whole human race. Considering further the oneness of the human race, it would stand to reason that all human individuals would unite in a universal political framework. However, after the great original migration, which took men out of their common birthplace and separated them into individual races, the distances involved were of such magnitude that they did not permit men to keep regular connections between the severed parts of the same human race. Primitive communication precluded the establishment of a universal political community. Therefore, ever since, men have lived in separate political communities which they established to serve their interests and altered according to their needs and their technical ability at a given time. All types of political communities as they appear successively on the scene of history are thus man-established, artificial and subject to transformation. The state, in all its historic forms, was only a makeshift substitute for the divinely-designed common political community of the whole human family.

As far as the individual's relation to the state is concerned, one ought never to lose sight of two facts. First, man is God's creation, whereas the state is only man's handiwork. This makes man, subject to God's design an end in himself, while the state remains only a means in man's hand. Secondly, the reason for the existence of the state is to serve the individual. Man established the state to serve his own interest. If the individual gave up some of his freedom, if he limited his sphere of action when he went into the state, he did it exclusively for his own sake in order to have his safety guaranteed and his well-being secured.

Since the state is artificial and since its mission is to serve the individual, it changes with the changing needs of the individual. Man-created things are not immutable. Even from the limited perspective of man's short recorded history, one can clearly distinguish a progressive variation in the form and type of man's political community.

Two basic trends connected with the fundamental aspirations of the individual find reflection in the progressive transformation of the state. One is the tendency toward extending human rights as well as assuring the means of sustenance to the masses. The other is the trend toward the gradual enlargement of the territorial base of the political community. Historic forces are driving man toward *democratization* and *territorial integration*. While backsliding is a common occurrence in history, from the vantage point of modern man these two trends appear clear.

Democratization has been an uneven and difficult process through the ages. The mission of the state to serve the interest of the individual could mean but one thing: to take into account equally and impartially the interests of *all* the individuals of which the community is composed. As a matter of fact, through history, more often than not, the state has ignored the interest of the greater part of its population as it has stood generally for the privileged few. To correct this situation, all through history, the abused masses have been striving to improve their lot. The trend toward democratization did not bring too much fruit before the beginning of the Christian era. It did, however, greatly influence man's history even before the coming of Christianity. Class-struggle was not unknown in the ancient times and all ages abound in rebellions of the oppressed. The variations in the form of state are partly explained by the trend of democratization and often reflect the result of a power struggle between social classes.

However, for our purposes, the important trend to consider

is the territorial integration. All the known historic types of state have clearly reflected this trend. The way to the modern nation-state leads from the family, clan, tribe through the city-state, kingdom, and empire. Who could deny that there is a gradually, if not evenly, enlarged territorial base involved in this transformation of man's political organization? The trend is definitely toward ever greater units and ultimately toward the reestablishment of man's original unity. This proves the transitoriness of whatever form the state takes in a given epoch. The average size of the territorial base of the state tends to grow on the way toward ultimate political unification. Because the state stands for the individual, who is a member of the human race, it has to enlarge its territory until it merges with the territory of the whole globe populated by men of the same family.

In order to see whether and when the process of integration will come to its logical conclusion by making the political community cover all the globe, we want to answer a decisive question. What were the factors determining the average size of the territory of the state at a given epoch of history? In other words, what were the factors that regulated and, in a sense, slowed down the process toward reintegration of the human race?

The average size of the state in a given era has depended on the development of the means of communication and transportation at that particular time. Technically speaking it has depended on the transportation radius calculated from the power-center of that community. With developing technical knowledge, greater territories became controllable from a given power-center. As the development of technological knowledge has been uneven, backsliding in territorial integration often occurred.

Whatever the average size of a political community, the important thing to bear in mind is the fact that the human race lived divided in political communities of limited size, not because the population of the then prevailing type of state represented a natural unit, which it never did, but because the size of the territory was restricted by the contemporary state of technology. Technology, up to our own day, did not permit the establishment of even continental units, let alone a universal political community. With developing technology, successively growing intercommunicable economic and cultural units were made possible. After a certain time-lag, correspondingly larger political units followed suit as logical consequence.

There is no reason why the state should not grow in size, once advance in communication permits or even necessitates such transformation. It is natural that as soon as a region, thanks to extended communication-radius, becomes intercommunicable and consequently transforms itself into an economic and cultural unit, it should also organize itself into a corresponding political entity, thus matching the economic and cultural realities.

Whereas developing technology brought with it the possibility of gradual extending the average size of man's political community, the direct cause behind the process of territorial integration was the changing need of the human individual. With human progress spurred by ever more intense intercommunication and furthered by the gradually growing sizes of political units, the personal requirements of the human individual were becoming more and more complex. The desire to satisfy man's diversified needs, in turn, again tended to extend man's economic and cultural sphere and to enlarge the territorial base of his political community. The result of this mutually stimulating relationship between man's need and the size of his political organization has expressed itself throughout history in the trend toward the enlarging of the average size of the state. This tendency was reenforced by the fundamental fact of the oneness of the human race; that is, by the consequent unconscious desire of man to bring ever greater numbers of people together in the same political framework, a fact which corresponds to an innate need of man to unite ultimately with all of his fellow-men.

As the human individuals are all alike, as they all are members of the same human race, and as they all were created by the same God, it is logical that ultimately they should tend to live all together in the same political framework. This is so even if human beings are not conscious of this trend. So long as technology did not permit such a solution, the tendency was to form states by bringing together the greatest possible number of people compatible with the technical development at the time. With technology becoming global, the oneness of the human race not only permits, but calls for, political unification on the global level.

With this trend in mind, does it not seem to run against the logic of history to see members of the same human race still living divided in artificial units in a time when technology has transformed the world into an economic unit and when the peoples of all continents are about to accept the same civilization?

If there is only one human race, is it not natural that the members of this one entity should try to build an all-inclusive political organization to cover their common needs? If, for particular purposes, local territorial organizations are legitimate, the solution of universal human problems requires the creation of a universal unit. Is not the natural human unit the universal?

To build a world organization is the only logical thing to do. It is the only way to establish lasting peace. It is the only way to get rid of the plague of war. The fratricidal stage of man's history will not come to an end until we establish a global organization able to adjust the conflicts which are bound to arise among coexisting people. It is as logical as it is natural that men who by the fact of their common origin belong to the same natural unit should have a political organization to take care of their multiplying common problems. During the time of relative separation, this was not possible, and it was not even necessary. In our day, since modern technical developments have made a completely interdependent and inter-communicative unit out of the world, it becomes both possible and necessary to erect a global political unit for all the members of the human race.

The reality of the oneness of the human race encourages man to hope for the coming of an institutionalized world community. The Christian's belief in the brotherhood of all men supports this hope.

2. WESTERN CIVILIZATION ENGULFS THE WORLD

In Chapter Two, under point two, we expressed our conviction that the regional civilizations never lost complete contact and that in the final account they were bound to contribute to the common progress of mankind.

However, the existence of regional civilizations with individual characteristics of their own and with distinct differences between them cannot be denied. In spite of their fundamental similarities, the individual regional civilizations all had their distinguishing cultures. Each worshiped different gods, each had its special spiritual values. Their economic, social and political institutions, though basically alike, differed in many respects. The men of each of the great regional civilizations had their own particular ways of life. Their ways of working and relaxing reflected the particular, often radically different, conditions under which they lived. Even their clothing was characteristically their own. General customs showed regional variations. In short, the fundamental oneness of the human race was hidden behind the many not fundamental, but very tangible, differences and particularities, which together make up the cultural heritage of an individual civilization.

The cultural characteristics link those who partake in the same individual civilization closely together. The aggregate of the commonly shared ideas and the uniform ways of life make the members of a cultural entity conscious of their common fate and destiny. This forges them into a sentimental unity. The likeness of spiritual values and material ways furthers the sentiment of belonging together and awakens the feeling of community in the men of the same civilization. On the other hand, it also accounts for the opposite feeling of being different from men of all other civilizations.

The feeling of belonging to a group of like persons creates not only a certain affection between them, but accounts for the loyalty to the group as a whole. Common cultural ties and the resulting common sentiments, expressed in community feeling, lead to the establishment of political community. This is because—although a common pattern of life, as a rule, assures peaceful social relations, for the adjustment of inevitable conflicts which are bound to arise among men living together—political authority has to be established. In turn, those who are heading the political community do their best to strengthen in the people the feeling of belonging together.

Thus, on the one hand it is natural that the community feeling, resulting from the commonly shared values and similar ways of life, leads to the creation of political community; on the other, it is also natural that political power, for the sake of self-perpetuation, is bound to strengthen the feeling of community in the minds of the subjects. If cultural differences are chiefly responsible for the division of the human race into regional civilizations, this division is considerably reinforced if the cultural unit happens to coincide with the political organization.

From what precedes, it would seem natural that political communities were always established on the base of cultural entities linking all the individuals of the same civilization under the same authority. In the past, this was not always the case. Culture could spread further than political power could extend its control. As the consequence, cultural communities were more often than not divided into several political states. There were, however, cases in which all members of the same civilization were united under the same political power. For instance, the Confucian civilization and the Chinese political empire tended through the ages to coincide. Less successful in this respect was the Hindu civilization. Hindu political power hardly ever succeeded in covering all the territories where the Hindu civilization prevailed. During the Christian Middle Ages the trend also was toward unifying under the same rule all peoples of Christian faith and culture. The desire to unite all Western Christians under the same scepter brought the Holy Roman Empire into being. While it might seem natural to want to gather all people of the same culture into one political fold, personal rivalry, family feuds and particularism played havoc most of the time with the principle that political power should coincide with an entire cultural region.

The fact that only seldom was it possible to establish empires to cover *all* people with the same culture does not contradict our belief that political communities, to be successful, had to link individuals of the same civilization. Although it was necessary to the survival of the state that the nationals shared the same civilization, it was not necessary that the state unite *all* the people who belonged to that particular civilization. As long as the members of the same state upheld the same ideals and followed the same way of life, the state's chances to survive were good, even if its authority did not cover everybody of the same civilization. The important thing was moral affinity and the sentimental attachment of the participants to each other.

As was the case most often in the past, our modern nation-states also divide men of the same civilization into separate political entities. We have many Christian, quite a few Moslem, and several Buddhist states, all of them politically subdividing their cultural unit. However, the base of the nation-state only seemingly is the language. The real connecting link is the special culture of the nation. Here too, the real tie is the belief in the same values, ideals and way of life. In a sense, special cultural subdivisions make the nation-states.

For our purpose, which is to look for the base on which to establish a universal political unit, the important thing is to know that in both cases—in the case of a regional empire, such as India is today, where a whole civilization forms the political community, and in the case of the nation-state, into which national segments of the same civilization are organized—we deal with men of the same general culture; that is, with people that share the same spiritual ideals and follow the same material way of life. Consequently the feeling of community in both cases exists, and it supports the state. (One of the important understandings of the Indian experience is the fact that India is composed of many language groups, which, should they become inspired by the

European type of language-nationalism, could form nation-states of their own. This would lead to the dissolution of the present Indian state.)

To weigh the chances of the coming of a universal political community we summarize what was said before. In order to establish any form of political community, it is necessary that the future members be linked by the feeling of community. This, in turn, can only rise in men if they actually belong to the same cultural unit. The future members of any political community to be established should uphold the same ideals and follow the same ways of life. They should be men of the same civilization. If we ever are to establish a universal political community, such an event has to be preceded by the fusion of the different cultural patterns into a universal one all over the world.

To properly appreciate the fundamental importance of the feeling of community we are going to relate it to such basic facts of our age as the oneness of the human race, the intense intercommunication among regions, the intermingling between men of different civilizations, and the economic interdependence of the world. Compelling as these most crucial facts are their warning to unite the whole human race will not be heeded without the rise of the feeling of human brotherhood.

In chapter two under point one we did indicate that our hope of establishing a world community is based, above all, on the fact of the oneness of the human race. Here we have to add that without community feeling among all men no global political community can be built. It is true that Christianity upholds the principle of common brotherhood. Science teaches the biological oneness of the human race. Still, as long as the deeply engrained cultural differences prevail between men and men, the general rise of the feeling of belonging to the same human race and sharing in the fate of all men will be retarded. This handicap will remain even if we should succeed in overcoming the obstacles presented by the nation-states, into which men of the individual civilizations are politically subdivided at the present. Cultural differences still would have to be faced and the great problem of fearing and distrusting men of different civilizations and races overcome.

Although, as we have seen, contacts never were completely severed between the individual civilizations, the desire to fuse all men into a greater unit never existed until the coming of our age. Only a few philosophers have dreamt about the reintegration of the human race. Meetings between men of different civilizations did not awake in their members the realization that all men belong to the same human race. It did not bring the feeling of common brotherhood to men. Not even with the coming of the intense intercommunication of our age did this situation change. If things changed, they seem, for the moment at least, have changed to the worse. The more intense the contact between regions of the world, the easier the exploitation of the less developed peoples; modern intercommunication has led to animosity between men of different civilizations, to racial conflicts, and to some inter-regional wars. The feeling of affection and the sentiment of affinity between all men is still to come.

Intercommunication is certainly a very important factor which not only facilitates but necessitates the establishment of a global political unit. However, inasmuch as only cultural affinity is apt to awake in men the feeling of belonging together, contacts between the different civilizations will not induce in them the feeling of community and will not lead them to desire to organize a global political community.

Nor did the modern universal intermingling between persons of different races with different cultural backgrounds fundamentally improve the situation in this respect. Direct daily personal contact between men of different culture, no matter whether resulting from permanent residence or from transitory business, did not necessarily teach them to love each other as members of the same human race. Knowing each other did not bring love toward each other. Not even has living together in the same political framework led necessarily to the amalgamation of the different groups. As long as they stick to their particular cultural heritage, they will only live beside each other but will not be fused into the same community. Political coexistence of men of different cultural backgrounds often even leads to mutual hatred and antagonism.

Different culture kept Hindus and Moslems of the Indian subcontinent apart for centuries and finally led to political separation. This ending was too bloody to be ignored. There are many groups of different cultural backgrounds surviving through many centuries in what are to them alien countries because of their adherence to some particular culture. We need only mention the case of the so-called "over-sea Chinese," who in the lands of their adoption generally defy all assimilation, not necessarily because of racial differences but because of their belonging to a separate cultural community. Such is the case with the Chinese of the countries in Southeast Asia. The survival of the Jewish people in so many different political units, a fact which borders on the miraculous, can also be explained by the fact that they stayed loyal to their ancient cultural heritage as perpetuated by their religion. We could multiply these examples if we had the space.

On the other hand, if men of different civilizations are willing to give up their own values and ways of life, the moment is bound to come when they will be absorbed completely into the body politic of their place of residence. The reason why the problem of the American Negro is not a really acute one is because he has accepted the American ideals and ways of life. Consequently, with certain qualifications, he feels part of the American community, which would not be the case if he did not share with his white partner the same ideals and ways of life. (Of course the only way to keep the Negro problem from boiling over is to help to develop further in them the feeling of community. This can come only if both whites and blacks live up to the ideals which they profess.)

Important as it is, not even the present economic interdependence of all the regions of the world can make the people realize the necessity of complete political cooperation. Compelling as its logic is in pointing to the necessity of world unification, grave as the consequences may be if its requirements are not followed by political action aiming at global integration, the fact of economic interdependence will not bring man necessarily closer to the solution of the grave problem of world organization. The pressure of economic reality will not necessarily bring the establishment of world community. It does little in itself to erase the differences between the cultural level of the different regions. It does not necessarily awake the feeling of community between men. It does not necessarily further the sentiment of common human fate. It does not necessarily create the feeling of human brotherhood nor bring about the rise of the belief in the oneness of the human race. It could do all these things if cultural and national differences would lose their importance or if all the cultures would fuse. On the other hand, as things stand today, economic interdependence has led more than once to economic conflicts and caused wars. It has also tempted Western man to exploit his less advanced fellow-men and subjugate them to his will.

In spite of the fact that all men belong to the same human race, in spite of the ever intensifying intercommunication between regions, in spite of more and more intermingling between men of different civilizations, and finally in spite of the economic interdependence of all nations, the chances of human reintegration will not be too bright until the feeling of belonging together and being members of the same human race becomes established in the hearts and minds of all men. This in turn can only come with the standardization of man's ideals and of his ways of life. The fusing of civilizations or the acceptance of one type of culture by all has to come before a universal political community can be established. This is the only way to awake the feeling of belonging to the same community in all men, which, we said, was the pre-condition of world unification. The enumerated factors have all contributed to make the world ripe for universal political organization, but to accomplish the fact the feeling of community has to rise in men.

But can men of one civilization accept the cultural standards of another civilization? Can individuals of the other civilizations make the Western ideals and Western ways their own? Can all men become partakers in a universal civilization?

All men, being members of the same human race, potentially are able to embrace any cultural standard. Men of other civilizations have fundamentally the same spiritual and intellectual capacity as the Western man and therefore can easily adopt the Western ideals and ways. No doubt, all men can be the carriers of a universal human civilization. History provides us with many examples of people of different civilizations having accepted entirely the culture of their neighbors, often of completely different racial and cultural background. Sometimes, the conquerors accepted the civilization of the conquered nation. In other instances, the culture of the victim went down and was replaced by the culture of the victor.

The acceptance of the same cultural values by all men is possible. The fusion of all civilizations is feasible. As a matter of fact, it is the pre-condition for the coming of a universal political community. Acceptance of the same civilization or merging of all civilizations is necessary.

Merging of the civilizations might come about by two ways. It could be brought about by the universal acceptance of Christianity, the base of Western civilization. Our spiritual ideals, like our material ways, are anchored on Christian standards. They evolved into what they are today in a Christian atmosphere and under Christian influence. With the acceptance of Christianity the rest of mankind would embrace the same ideals and consequently attain the like results. Christianity, universally accepted, would implant the feeling of love toward each other into the hearts of all men and it could not help but open the way toward political world unity.

However, looking at things from the very limited perspective of human understanding, it does not seem now that the fusion of the different civilizations would come about through the acceptance of Christianity by the non-Christian part of the human race. There are no earthly indications that Christianity will be brought to all men in our life-time. However, things of the spirit are beyond all comprehension.

Acceptance of one type of civilization also can be brought

143

about in the reverse. Western material standards could be taken over without the acceptance of the spiritual base of Western civilization: Christianity.

As a matter of fact, this is what is happening. We are witnessing a uniformization of civilization. A new universal civilization seems to be in the process of becoming. This is happening by the acceptance of the Western ways of living and doing things. Gradually our technological civilization is engulfing the globe.

This process started with the colonization of the countries of Asia and Africa. Western man did not intend to spread his civilization to the "heathens," he only wanted to use the newly occupied territories for his own sake. However, as it happened, the exploitation of the colonies could only be achieved by Western ways and methods. New ways of agriculture were introduced in the colonies, plantations with Western ways of cultivation were set up. Roads and rail-roads had to be built to transport the crop to the next harbor. Ports were needed for transporting raw-material to the West. Centers of trade and transportation and naval bases were constructed. At a later stage, Western man penetrated deep into the inland of the colonies to exploit the rich mineral resources there. New territories had to be consolidated and administered, if for no other reason than to secure the peaceful exploitation of the colonies and to guarantee constant and dependable local labor for the white man. While industrialization was not intended, mills were erected in many instances for turning the bulky raw-material into easier transportable half-finished goods, and small factories were built for the processing of perishable food. Although Western man was not too much concerned with the illiteracy of the natives, elementary skills were taught to improve the quality of the local man power. Western conscience was not totally dormant. Missionaries were sent to the colonies; schools and hospitals were built, sanitation introduced. The last thing the European master originally wanted was to give political rights to the people; still, with the rise of democracy in the mother countries, the time came when very gradually steps were taken to introduce self-government in some of the colonial countries. Although

144

all this was not too much in the way of westernization, some sectors of the native population did get in touch with the Western way of life, and did accept Western ways. Especially such was the case with the well-to-do, who sent their sons and daughters to Europe and to the United States for education.

While this spotty and limited westernization of the colonial countries was only the by-product of western exploitation, it was none-the-less real and important for the future developments. The situation radically changed with the rising tide of nationalism in Asia and Africa. The liberation movements were mostly led by Western educated persons. Here we include the Bolshevik agitators, or those who received their education in Soviet Russia. After all, communism is a Western product itself, put in practice by a Christian nation of Caucasian race.

The Asian revolt against the so-called colonial powers is in its last phase. Most, if not all, of the Asian nations have regained their independence. The peoples of Africa are also rising and are in the process of gaining their freedom. Some of them have already succeeded in this endeavor, others are still fighting for it. It is by no means unimportant for our purpose to remember that Western ideas caused these revolutionary changes in the political status of Asia and Africa. Western ideas acted as a ferment to stir up the desire of the natives to become free. Western patterns were used in the revolt themselves. Western knowledge and Western means enabled the colonial peoples to succeed in their fight for independence. Western standards and ways were also employed when it came to the actual setting up of the new governments. The very idea of nationalism, which started the whole process, was taken over by the peoples of the East from the West. The impact of Western civilization made them stand up and fight for their rights.

Once independent, the new Asian and African nations are dead set to get rid of their backwardness and of their misery. They desire to raise the living standard of their peoples and to modernize their lives. They know that the only way to attain these purposes is to learn the Western ways. They all are embarked on the great venture to transform their countries into Western-type states. If in the colonial times Western ways were brought to them, today they do their very best themselves to catch up with the Western man in the material sense.

The newly established countries might differ in whether they adhere to the communist ideology or follow the democratic way of life, but they are all alike in their aspiration to westernization in general and in their ambition for quick industrialization in particular. Although the means employed to reach this goal are different in democratic India from those used by communist China, both governments are doing their very best to attain the high material standard of the West. In their craving to forge ahead as fast as possible, the less developed countries not only follow Western procedures and use Western techniques, they are more than willing to accept any direct material or intellectual help the West or the Soviet can offer, provided that no strings are attached. As illustrations to this point we cite the United States Point Four Program, the British-initiated Colombo Plan, the United Nations Technical Assistance Program and the recent Soviet offers to help the Arab and other Asian nations.

In the course of the last few years, since the liberation, truly great achievements have been made in the material sense. Most of the new governments have made a very good start in modernizing, that is westernizing, their countries.

Their political institutions are patterned on the white man's model, be it the democratic model of the "West" or the totalitarian pattern of the Soviet Union. The same applies to the final transformation of the economic and social structure of these countries, which also follows modern lines.

Besides modernizing their countries in the material sense, the peoples of Asia and Africa are also in a state of intellectual fermentation. Here too, the stimulation comes from the West of the white man, including the Soviet empire. The people in general are well informed about current events of importance. They are keeping abreast of all the new developments in the Western world. Their interests are stirred by the same things as ours, the routine of their very personal lives reflects the modernization of their countries. They tend to accept ever more Western habits and Western ways. With westernized economics, and with technology taking over the Eastern man is changing even to the point of accepting Western clothing and Western ways of relaxation. He participates more and more in the problems of our interdependent world.

As far as ideals and moral values are concerned (which make up in the narrow sense the intangible part of a civilization referred to as culture), here too, great changes are in the offing. The same type of schooling and general education cannot but spread the same ideas. Global news-exchange services, radio, newspapers, propaganda, student and teacher exchanges, assistance programs, international conferences, foreign travels, military service abroad, these all tend to erase ultimately the differences between the ideas of men of different civilizations. The common sources of information, and the global character of their news-coverage, are bound more and more to affect uniformly people's minds all over the world. With all the means of intercommunication, with all of the intermingling of men of different regions and with all of the many other varied types of international contacts multiplying day by day, a leveling process between men of different civilizations is going on even in the cultural sense. Western science, philosophy, literature, and art exercise a decisive influence on the Eastern mind. Not even the influence of the Western movies can be discounted. The ideological war between the communist and the democratic halves of the world —a struggle which started within the fold of the same Western civilization—is also fought out before a global audience, with special attention to the Eastern mind.

The total effect of all these factors is the gradual standardization of man's thoughts and his cultural values. In this standardization the giver is mostly the West. The intellectual, moral amalgamation, affecting all the nations, is equivalent to the spreading of the Western civilization all over the globe. This does not mean that the West itself is not greatly affected by this cultural fusion.

As the consequence of accepting Western ways, material,

147

intellectual, and moral, the people of the East and South are weakening the spiritual bonds which attach them to their ancient gods. The old honored religions of the East are in danger of withering away. Hinduism, Buddhism, even Islam (though in a much lesser way), which not so long ago permeated the total life of the peoples of Asia, are gradually losing their hold on the nations of the East. As the culture of the Asians has been based on their great religions, with the crumbling of the cultural superstructure it seems that the religious foundation itself is losing its reason for existence. With the discarding of the old cultural standards, the whole religious base is shaking. The ancient gods are becoming useless, it seems. The people are gradually forgetting them. The problem of the spiritual vacuum so created has sinister implications.

But is not the situation, in this respect, the same in the West? Did the Western man not discard his God also, when he de-spiritualized and de-Christianized his thought and life? There is a fundamental difference between the two cases. It is true, the cultural super-structure of the Western civilization was built on the foundation of Christianity, just as the cultural super-structure of the Asians was based on their respective religions. It is also true that both the West and the East seem to worship material gods presently. However, there are important differences. The Western man might have de-Christianized his culture, he might have cast away Christianity for the moment, he might have even denied his God. This does not change the basic connection between Western man's civilization and Christianity. Moreover, Western man did not sever all connections with Christianity, which remains the base of the material part of his civilization. Still Christianity is with him. Christianity is taught in the churches and in the schools. Christianity, even in its institutionalized form, remains a most vital force in the West. Consequently, should Western culture run into trouble, should Western political or economic institutions need to be reformed, Western man could turn with confidence for help to Christianity. The cultural super-structure of the Western civilization is based on Christianity, as we have said, and it is natural to turn for help to the faith which inspired the rise of that civilization.

As civilization in general is based on religion, the connection between the two is most vital in the survival of a civilization. It is also crucially important for the solution of cultural, political and economic troubles which arise within any community. The non-Christian nations are now in a process of accepting a culture which arose in the Christian West and is based on a faith which is alien to them now. In vain would they turn for help to their ancient gods, should anything go wrong with the civilization which they are in a process of embracing. The ideas, values and ways of life they are making their own now have no connections with their old religions. The only faith to which the people of the East could turn, in case of adversity, with complete trust in the forthcoming help, is Christianity.

Meanwhile, the material part of Western civilization is engulfing the globe. The gradual unification of the different civilizations is in progress. What we are witnessing in our day is the fusion of the different currents of regional civilizations into a mighty stream of unified human civilization. We are standing by the cradle of the reintegration of the human race. The sun of universal civilization is about to appear on the horizon. With the arising uniform cultural standard will end the fear of the "alien" which fills the hearts of men of different civilization. With the standardization of cultures will come the feeling of universal brotherhood, and the understanding of the reality of the oneness of the human race. The feeling of community among all men will come. This, in turn, is the pre-condition of the establishment of a universal political commonwealth bringing together the whole human race into a global political community.

3. *PROGRESS LIES ON THE PATH OF TERRITORIAL INTEGRATION*

We expressed our confidence in man's ability to progress in the second chapter under point three. It may be hard to perceive the slow forward movement of man if we look only into the mirror of recorded history, for its annals cover only about ten thousand years compared with the many millions of years of man's existence. However, if we consider man's story as reconstructed by the archeologists, from the dawn of time, with primitive man rising and setting out on his career, we can have no doubt that man, with the help of his Creator, has succeeded in making considerable progress and has lived up to his earthly mission of striving toward self-perfection.

But, even if we restrict our vision to recorded history, we need not deny man's capacity to progress. We believe progress is the result of the interplay of the achievements of the different nations, regions, and civilizations. Considering the picture of human civilization as a whole, we are able to perceive how man is slowly climbing the rock of human progress. This is particularly visible since the coming of and as the consequence of, Christianity. Looking at history from the inspired perspective of Christianity man's ability to progress is clearly reflected on its pages. In the course of the last five hundred years great progress has been made on the road of democratization and not less success has been scored in the field of technology.

However, the political progress of the West was and still is confined to national politics. The international scene, the relations between nations, remain anarchic. Many think that man has reached the limit of his political progress. They doubt man's ability to overcome the limitations of narrow minded nationalism. They do not believe that man will ever be able to make the next step on the road to territorial integration. Therefore it is necessary to examine whether we can hope that man will be able to build bigger political units than the present nation-states. Let us see whether we can hope for still greater progress by building a global unit.

If there has been noticeable progress in technological, economic, social, and political values since the great gift of Christianity was offered to mankind, there has also been a continuous forward march in the process of territorial integration. This march had, indeed, begun even prior to the coming of Christianity. If history teaches anything, it teaches the great lesson of territorial integration. Small units are giving way to ever-growing and more powerful political structures. As the needs of humanity are multiplying, as the economic interdependence between groups of nations is becoming more and more commanding, as technology more and more links all the different regions of the world, the need for uniting more and more people within the same political organization becomes ever more intensely felt. Recorded history testifies to the continuous process of territorial integration.

Why should we imagine that this process of integration has stopped for good? What reason do we have for supposing that this process of building ever greater territorial units came to an end with the creation of the national state? Why should we suppose that the political intelligence of man became sterile after it brought about the idea of nationalism? Although fanatics of nationalism think and act as though the national state were here to stay, and though the stubbornness of these sovereigns of the present international scene is in great measure responsible for the impasse in international relations, why should we suppose that we will stop halfway on the road to territorial integration?

We who believe in progress deny the inevitability of stopping short of our aim: the unification of all nations in one political unit. This would be against all reason. It would be against the lesson of history.

History teaches us that whenever the necessity of creating a bigger political unit presented itself the concerned group of individuals were, as a rule, ready to accept the new political form. They were not only ready, but Providence provided them with such an elementary force of conviction about the necessity of the change that no force of conservatism or reaction was strong enough to withstand the pressure of the accumulated energies working towards the creation of the next larger form of political unit.

Sometimes it was force which built the next unit in the trend of political territorial integration. Sometimes it was the enthusiasm of the concerned group of people. Even in the cases when force did the uniting, if the time was ripe for the next step the new political organization then was sanctioned by the people because it corresponded to their growing needs for well-being and security.

History provides us with many examples to prove that once powerful basic ideals, which were adhered to for long centuries when they provided the cement to hold political units together, fell into disrepute and lost their vitality as changed conditions and new needs made newly-risen ideas more attractive and inspiring.

We know, for instance, that the idea of Italian and German nationalism is relatively new. The Italians and Germans were divided into many small kingdoms, principalities, and city-states. The Germans and Italians, like the people of many other nations before their ultimate unification was accomplished, fought each other in innumerable fratricidal wars. Bavaria, Prussia and the other German states often allied themselves with non-German nations to fight against their German brothers. Bavarian loyalty, similar to the loyalty of the Venetian to his glorious republic, lasted for many centuries. It provided these people with emotional drives to accomplish great deeds. However, once the necessity for these smaller sovereignties was lost, their vitality also was gone. Once a bigger unit promised a better future, nothing could stop them from fading away. No army could save them, and no command could preserve the loyalty and attachment of their devotees. As soon as a new idea, representing a more progressive form of political co-operation and leading to the next forward step in the process of territorial integration rose on the horizon, the masses began to lose their enthusiasm for the old ideals. They were ready to give up their old loyalty and exchange it for the new one. With swelling hearts and boundless enthusiasm they greeted the rising sun.

The intense national loyalty of our days was unknown to men of the past. The loyalty to the sovereign or to the dynasty was the cement holding together what was then considered the state. Inspired by their intense loyalty towards their sovereign, people gladly gave their lives for him on whom they depended. The ties connecting the subjects of the same sovereign often cut across linguistic units, separating them into different and often antagonistic states. In feudal times the basis of political unification was the economic dependence of the subjects upon the sovereign.

In spite of the strength of the feudalistic system and the force of the vested interests involved, changing times and new needs produced a new central idea, nationalism, which took over in Europe. The new idea broke all resistance and swept victoriously all over the continent. The previous conceptions of state loyalty were blown away. Not much remained of loyalty to the sovereign or to the particular local unit.

When the time is ripe, when a new idea is taking hold of men, no force of the past, no ideal of bygone times is strong enough to stand in its way. Victory marches with progress. Reaction, in the long run, always will be defeated. The successive steps of territorial integration were made because they were needed. They could not be held up. When the time becomes ripe, old political forms are discarded and new ones are then embraced.

Some may object that this time it will be different. They might submit that the achievements of the national state are such that the attachment of the citizens toward the national state will outlive the usefulness of this "new" political organization. Many feel that nationalism has become such a force that it cannot be challenged. Man thinks of himself as being foremost an American, or a German, or a Hungarian. He has hardly any awareness of being part of the great natural community of mankind. Many question whether man will be able to break through the wall of all of the impediments which stand in the way of further unification.

But history offers a ray of hope. Was it not much harder for prehistoric man to overcome his natural impulse to grab everything for himself? Was it not harder for primitive man to overcome his egoistic instincts which led him into a permanent fight with his neighbors? Does it not seem much more difficult to understand how he could renounce his unsocial habits and form an organized community? Was it not more of an accomplishment to come out of the cave and stop "the fight of everybody against everybody," as it is described by Hobbes? Was it not much more difficult for the individual to ascend the hill towards organized society? Was it not a much greater achievement for man to take the momentous step of breaking the deadlock of anarchy in the relations of individual human beings? Was it not more difficult to build the first state? Is it not much more difficult to win over our individual egoism? Is it not harder to overcome the impulses of our ego? Is it not much harder to give up the self-centered approach of our narrow-minded individualism?

The greatest political achievement of man was scored when he realized that in order to survive and to progress he must unite into groups of co-operative members.

We have to stress the infinite difficulty of this first step because of the encouragement it offers for us today, when we are anxious to see the next step taken toward the realization of the coming political pattern of human co-operation. Without question the first step towards human political organization was the hardest. Never did the bringing about of the next step of integration involve the same measure of self-victory as did the momentous first one, the establishment of the first political community.

While in each of the later integrations one brand of community feeling had to be substituted for another—that is, the feeling of loyalty towards a previous existing unit had to be replaced by a similar feeling towards the newly-created organization—the first integration involved something more difficult; it meant self-renunciation, which affected the primary instinct of the individual himself. In the initial integration, that of renouncing the fight of every individual against every other individual, the very control of the elementary drives of the individual himself was set in operation. In all the rest, only the feeling of loyalty to one form of community had to be transferred to another. Only collective, not individual, feeling was involved.

It is bound to remain the greatest political mystery how man, as a member of human society, could have overcome his instinct of thinking and acting under the impulse of the moment and how he could have accepted the organized community and, later, have built the state. It will probably always remain unexplained how it happened that stupid limitations, imposed by basic selfishness, gave way to what we today would call the enlightened self-interest of man. We cannot but believe that it was the divine spark which ignited the flame that made the necessary transformation of man possible to enable him to solve an apparently insoluble problem.

If recorded history does not go back far enough to enlighten man on the problem of how organized political coexistence came about, it does go back far enough to illustrate the successive steps of territorial integration. As time marched on, further integrations, involving larger and larger human groups, became necessary. As successive integrations lighted the path of progress and as greater and greater units were formed, the story repeated itself. The old loyalty and the old allegiance had to be broken. The spell of the old gods had to be lifted. The different, outmoded patterns of territorial integration all fell along the roadside in due time. The next step could never be taken prematurely. But when the fulness of time was at hand, nobody and nothing could hold back the next step of human integration.

While this is true, it is also true that history's progress as revealed in successive territorial integrations was neither even nor uninterrupted. One region might have seen a more progressive political form of integration arise well ahead of some other part of the world. Other regions might have lagged well behind. Neither was it unusual that in the same region different types of territorial authorities coexisted. Reverses in history have been frequent. Progress never can be expected to be uninterrupted. Forms of political organizations fell and reappeared with dismaying irregularity.

It remains true that new ideas, if they are progressive, can only be retarded temporarily. They cannot be held back permanently. They appear to have faltered, and they might have fallen, but they gave way only to reappear so much more vigorously and to take over victoriously in due time. Progress can take defeat. It can stand to be defeated, because it carries within it the seeds of final victory. It is bound to try again and again, for final success is assured from the start. In the moment of death, the eyes of the martyrs in the great human causes flash once more with the certainty of coming victory for the ideal for which they gave their lives.

The pattern of territorial integration, in very rough outline, has been this. The first loyalty attached members of the same family together. This was succeeded by a feeling of allegiance toward the tribe, which form survives even today. City-states and kingdoms arose as a possible next step. Traces of their ancient glory linger on. Great self-motivated empires followed in turn. Their ambitious leaders glorified themselves, inspired by greed and hunger for power. The process of empire-building was tried again in our day and has failed. The idea of democratic national states of different size is still very much alive today. They occupy a considerable part of the globe. They too will have to give way before the next step on the road of territorial integration. Already experimentation is going on toward the final integration of mankind. Unfortunately false doctrines are being propagated and they endanger the work of the really democratic reintegration of mankind.

Will human community feeling in man ever be strong enough to overcome the ties attaching the individual to other less integrated human collectivities? We can better understand the gravity of this question and be in a better position to venture an answer if we try to re-examine the problem of nationalism. Without question, nationalism is one of the chief obstacles today in the way of human community feeling.

Nationalism came as an inspiration to restrain former loyalties of more primitive types. It came also to restrain, as far as it was possible, the remnants of man's egoistic drives, surviving in spite of all the succeeding historic forms of integration. Prior to the rise of modern nationalism, the world never knew such intensity in political loyalty as has been created by the exigencies of the national state. Man never before gave up voluntarily so much of his individuality and of his innate rights as he has done since the coming of modern nationalism. Nationalism was the means that accomplished the change towards the next step of political development. Nationalism was the inspiration that built and has kept going the presently all-powerful unit, the sovereign national state. Nationalism not only brought a new and more advanced form of integration. It also meant a more intense voluntary attachment of the individual to the existing highest political unit. Some scholars such as Hans Morgenthau explain the intensity of modern nationalism by assuming that, since nationalism dominates man's thinking, man transforms his own impulses into collective ones. According to them, man's individual impulses dissolve into collective national drives. Modern man, according to this school of thought, effectuates his personal impulses by passionately embracing the collective cause of his country and by fervently sharing in the excitement of undertakings for national aggrandizement, advance, enrichment, and victory. A nationalist does not hate his personal enemies the most; he hates the enemies of his nation above all. He gladly applauds the achievements of his neighbors, but he envies intensely the accomplishments of his country's rivals. He kills not for personal reason, but for the glory of his fatherland. Nationalism, thus conceived, is a collective drive. As collective inspirations represent the aggregation of the drives of the component individuals, their intensity is immense.

Whether we accept this theory or not, it is true that collective inspirations exist only in sofar as they are the composite total of the individual inspirations of the members of the group. As a certain collective unit exists only because of the group of individuals who comprise it, collective inspirations have independent existence only as the sum of the inspirations of the members. Group units, collective entities, being as they are artificial organizations, cannot have any direct impulses. Nationalism is the collectively felt sentiment of the individuals who form the nation and uphold the national state. The national state itself is but the institutionalization of the inspiration of nationalism.

The force of the inspiration, embedded in a collective human unit but based on the emotions and sentiments of the member-individuals, is immense. The greater the unit, the greater technically is the force which it is bound to create. Numbers represent hard facts, not to be disregarded, though many other factors contribute to make power.

The accomplishments of modern nationalism are great. Nationalism was a step forward, when it appeared upon the scene. The role it played in bringing about modern democracy was of utmost importance. However, its days are numbered because a new form of integration is in the offing. A new form of political organization is waiting to have its turn. It cannot be delayed.

As soon as one form of political grouping outgrows its usefulness for the individual human being, it can no longer stand in the way of further integration. The integration process has to go on in the interest of the collectivity, made up of each and every individual human being.

How about the chances of the new inspiration just coming over the horizon to create the next, possibly ultimate human integration? Should we suppose that the uninterrupted succession of integrations will end now, long before all of the units have been integrated? Would it not be unnatural to suppose that a process which during millenniums of human history has been going on with such relentlessness, should stop now without reaching its logical end? Why should we think that the present form of human political integration will last forever? Why should we suppose that man's forward march should stop with the status quo and that his political achievements will fossilize in their present stage? Why should history change its logic?

Why should the rules be changed in the middle of the game? Why should we at this point lose our faith in God, who has helped us to progress so far? Why should we be overcome by defeat now, after we have been victorious with God's help in so many hard-fought battles of man's story?

We know that standing motionless is not possible. We know that not to progress is to decay and to die. Why should we not be optimistic as to our chances of making the next step on the way toward integration?

True, nationalism as the prevailing inspiration of the present form of political integration is a tremendous force. There is no use denying that nationalism, as a collective inspiration, presently is consuming the greatest part of the drives and emotions of the individual human beings who all live in one or another form of national sovereign state. But, is nationalism not based on the feelings of the individuals? And is the interest of the individual human being completely served by the present artificial form of political organization built by individuals, the sovereign national state?

Do we not see signs of impending catastrophe if we do not change our course in international relations? Do we not see signs that growing numbers of individuals are attracted by the new ideal of universal human co-operation, just because they want to save themselves? Do we not sense that millions are losing their faith in the old, rigid, and out-dated forms of political organization? Do we not see the handwriting on the wall, warning us concerning the fate of our civilization and of ourselves, if we do not heed the lesson of history? Are we unable to see that the hands of the clock again have moved and that a new and all-powerful inspiration is about to emerge?

Why should we not believe that the new inspiration will have its way, as have all of the foregoing inspirations that have heralded successive human integrations? Why should we doubt that the rising inspiration, that of universal integration, will be strong enough to challenge the old? Why should we suppose that nationalism will be spared the fate of the preceding inspirations?

Nationalism is only one of the many inspirations on the historic road towards ever more complete human integrations. It was not the first one, and it will not be the last. It had its chance and it used it well. It was undoubtedly necessary that it appear on the way towards political progress. Its accomplishments are truly great. Even today nationalism is playing an important role in colonial or former colonial countries. In these areas of political backwardness nationalism still helps to build democracy as it helped to establish democracies in the course of the nineteenth century.

Just as nationalism was vital in its time of usefulness and just as it was strong enough to accomplish its historic mission, so will the next human inspiration on the road toward further integration be strong enough to bring about the final territorial integration. Just as the former allegiances were ultimately too weak to stand in the way of emerging nationalism, so is nationalism today bound to recede before the tide of the oncoming wave of universal co-operation.

Here, then is our conclusion under this heading. In terms of universal humanity we see progress in man's political life. We have reason to think that this forward march, which consists in meeting new situations and in satisfying new needs as they arise, will not stop. The further integration of the human race cannot be halted. A global organization of all the people of the world, representing the interest of all, is bound to emerge sooner or later.

4. SPECIAL QUALIFICATIONS ENABLE
THE WORLD TO ORGANIZE

In chapter two, under point four, we enumerated the differences between our civilization and the preceding ones. These are the differences on which we based the assertion that the West holds special qualifications for the survival of its civilization. Let us now re-examine the advantages our age possesses with a view toward estimating the chances of the final integration of mankind.

The weapons that supported us in our fight for survival, the means that enabled us to solve the problems of an ever-changing world, the forces that made our progress possible, are Christianity, democracy, and technology. This is the sequence in which they arose. Their inter-relationship is established: Christianity was needed to develop democracy as democracy was needed to bring about modern technology. One cannot be a democrat without being Christian, that is, without accepting Christian social standards. One cannot understand the rise of modern technological civilization without appreciating the decisive role that democracy played in its building. How could technological progress be brought about without freedom of mind, freedom of research, freedom of education, and even freedom of religion—that is, without democracy? Modern technology never would have been born in the dark atmosphere of ignorance or under the shadows of superstition, characteristic of political oppression and despotism.

For our present purpose the most important point in the relationship of Christianity, democracy, and technology is this: Christianity not only was needed to bring about democracy, and democracy was not only necessary to create the proper atmosphere for the germination of technology. Their relation is not only that of genetics.

Democracy not only presupposes the prior existence of

161

Christianity. It postulates Christianity not only during the germination period, but its further existence also depends on Christianity as long as it exists. The very continuity of democracy requires Christian atmosphere. Christianity does not alone act as a creative agency for democracy; democracy could not even survive without Christianity.

The relation between technology and democracy likewise is not only genetic. The atmosphere of democracy indeed was needed to bring modern technology. However, not only the germination but also the continued existence of technology calls for democratic conditions.

Thus, the three are parts of a successive evolution which results in steady progress. They are steps of the same stairway. How can the higher stepping-stone hold, if the preceding ones collapse? Technology cannot stand if democracy and Christianity, or either of the two, are eliminated.

As far as our present problem is concerned, the question of the possibility of uniting the human race in a political framework, the point made above is of crucial importance. While means of technology are enabling man to unify the world, without democracy and without Christianity he would not have a chance to succeed in this undertaking. It is true that a world-commonwealth depends on technology to survive, but would a world organization based on technology not destroy itself if democracy should be discarded? Or, could a global commonwealth have a chance to remain democratic if Christianity did not inspire it?

If we want to succeed in erecting a world authority and if we wish to see it endure, we have to be conscious of the exact relationship of Christianity, democracy, and technology. We have to realize that not only are all three needed to build a world-commonwealth, but that the continued existence of all the three is necessary to the survival of such an organization.

In the third chapter, in which we described one by one the five special qualifications of our age, we could not help but touch on the problem of how Christianity, democracy, technology, and the awakening world-consciousness could help man erect a global world community. It is time now to pursue this problem and make some additional points.

Not much is left to add to the importance of technology as a basic factor in the possible building of a world-commonwealth. No authority disputes the crucial role which technology played in transforming the basic relationship of the nations, to a point where the need for further territorial integration is most keenly felt. Few would deny the primary role to technology in the building of a peaceful and prosperous world. However, as far as democracy and Christianity are concerned we will have to add some specific remarks.

Democracy's significance for the shaping of the future of the nations does not only come from its close relation to technology as we recognized before. Its importance as a factor in erecting and sustaining an organized world order is not only indirect. Democracy's role is direct inasmuch as a world-commonwealth would have no chance to be built and to survive unless it was erected on democratic principles. All the attempts of the past to build world empires failed because they were not based on democratic ideals, but were motivated by the desire to dominate and exploit subjected peoples. One of the most important reasons for hope of the termination of the international impasse of our age is the belief that international democracy is on the rise. International democracy postulates equality for all peoples and rejects all discrimination among them. Accordingly, if ever a global commonwealth is to be erected, it will have to be built by all of the nations and in the interest of all the peoples of the world. Within its framework the democratic principle would not admit the subjection or exploitation of any nation or any race. In it, there could be no ruling nation or ruling class. Such an organization would exist for the sake of all of the peoples that would unite in it. Without international democracy the different nations would not be willing to join and, if forced into it, would sooner or later overthrow it.

The accepted close inter-relationship between Christianity, democracy, and technology, with the latter two depending on the first, should be actually sufficient proof to Christianity's importance for the establishment and support of a world-commonwealth. Since Christianity is the basis of democracy, and since technology depends on democracy, the two latter never could have developed without Christianity, and thus never could have brought about the present state of international affairs which not only makes the erecting of a universal political organization possible but which actually necessitates the building of such a human unit. If established, a world-commonwealth could not long endure should Christianity be abandoned. For in such a case democracy would be bound to wither away and technology, in turn, would destroy itself.

Beyond this indirect importance, Christianity's paramount importance for the elimination of the international impasse and the opening of the road toward future integration lies in its spiritual inspiration. Christianity has a most crucial direct role to play in bringing about the awareness of human community. Only by sharing Christian spiritual standards can we secure the desired cultural uniformity among men of all regions that is necessary for the growth of the awareness of human unity which is a prerequisite to the political fusion of all nations and all races.

As we have seen, the awareness of human community can be brought about by the fusion of temporal ideals and ways of life. However, without the acceptance of uniform spiritual values based on identical faith, such formal amalgamation of man's cultural standards cannot fully guarantee the endurance of the political fusion which would follow. The awareness of human unity which is necessary to build a universal political organization will endure only if the amalgamation of values includes also the fusion of views about transcending problems and of spiritual values. This in turn, can only be brought about by universal acceptance of the same faith. As we consider Christianity the only perfect answer to man's most sublime aspirations, we believe that only Christianity can provide man with the needed spiritual foundation on which to erect a uniform cultural super-structure.

Our specific reason for believing in Christianity's universal calling to implant in all human beings the feeling of human community is the fact that the ideal of the brotherhood of all men is one of its main tenets. This ideal, if accepted universally, cannot help but awaken in all men the awareness of common human destiny and unity. One cannot overestimate Christianity's importance in this respect. The command that we should love *all* our neighbors as ourselves, has already worked wonders. Even in a religiously divided world, the idea of respect for all human individuals, irrespective of race, nationality, or color, is spreading all over the world. This is definitely a Christian achievement. In a cultural sense it is probably the most momentous achievement of our time. The fusing of cultural standards all over the world, a process which we are witnessing today, cannot safely be carried out and cannot lead to enduring universal political organization unless it is inspired by Christian faith.

At this point it would be encouraging to listen to Saint John quoting the Christ:

"And other sheep I have, which are not of this fold: them also I must bring, and they shall hear my voice; and there shall be one fold, and one shepherd."

*   *   *   *

The reader will permit a digression here. Although the point which we desire to make does not fit neatly into the framework of what we have just been saying, it is closely related to the subject.

Apart from Christianity, democracy, technology, and world consciousness there is a further factor which could give us hope that, once established, a democratic world-commonwealth would stand an incomparably better chance to survive and to stay secure than has any previous regional empire.

The fact that our civilization is global or is gradually becoming global makes all the difference for its survival. The fall of great civilizations, that is, the fall of the political organizations supporting them, was caused mostly by internal weakness and degeneration. However, the final blow, not only to their political existence but to their culture, came mostly from outside. After the inner proletariat turned away from the ideals they represented, the outside proletariat—in the case of Rome, the Germanic tribes—finished the job.

The future of an empire, and of its civilization, is never secure until all neighboring territories are brought under control. All empires strive to subjugate the nations living outside their territories in order to assure complete security from outside attack. Even the most backward outside tribal forces can turn into dangerous aggressors with the weakening of the empire. No assurance of permanent peace and security exists for an empire and the culture it represents until the whole world is brought under its control.

Should one world empire be realized, it will have more chance of survival than any great regional empire of the past ever had. This is because no possible aggressors will be left outside of its boundaries to threaten it. The only peril—as far as outside aggressors are concerned—would have to come from "outer space." And such a danger is purely hypothetical.

PART THREE

CHAPTER V

DANGERS OF A TECHNOLOGICAL AGE

1. PITFALLS OF MATERIALISM

The fundamental trouble of our time is the fact that we have become worshippers of material values. We look at science, the explainer and employer of material forces, as an end in itself. We look at it (and this seems to be a contradiction) as the key to the solution of all our problems. We neglect spiritual values. We look at technology, which in a material sense is based on science, as the essence of our modern Western civilization. We think that technology itself can make man happy and can fulfill all his aspirations.

However, there are some who sense what would happen if we should forget the spiritual foundation of technology. They know that it would fall and that its perishing would bring crashing down the many important material values that we cherish. They know that technology without the inspiration of democracy and Christianity would be certain to free some terrible, destructive forces and would endanger and eventually destroy civilization. Recent history should be a warning to this effect.

In the early decades of capitalism, technology without democracy, without the participation of the common man in the direction of his own destiny, had meant not only exploitation of the individual human being; it meant also the humiliating degradation of man.

Without democratic constitutional guarantees, the masses would be dispossessed, as they once were and as they still are in countries without democracy. All the human rights that are inherent in human beings according to Christianity preclude the economic exploitation of man by man. They preclude the degradation of man because he is a divinely created being. Without democracy the profiteers of modern technology would enchain the masses, and they would debase themselves by doing so. They would become soul-less human molochs of self-enrichment. They would lose all spiritual aspirations and would degenerate themselves to egoistic and power-hungry slaveholders. Materialistic society would ultimately dig its own grave.

Technology also can make even greater the existing social and economic differences between man and man. It can help to discriminate against the weak. It may deepen the gulf separating man from man. A purely technological world, in this sense, means a materialistic world where only money and what money represents are of value.

At the dawn of the nineteenth century, all these dangers were very real. Only democracy could save mankind from such a dismal fate. Only democracy, based on Christianity, lifted man's soul again towards values higher than material goods. Only democracy was able to lead Western mankind out of the desert of class hatred, egoism, and exploitation.

While on the one hand the atmosphere of the nineteenth century materialism was responsible for the growth of selfish, uncontrolled capitalism with all its un-Christian vices, on the other hand this same atmosphere also favored the rise of an ideology which did not hesitate to make a frontal attack on Christianity itself. We mean Marxism. This pretendedly progressive ideology, which promised to lead the oppressed and exploited proletariat from their underprivileged position, also emphasizes the importance of technology, just as capitalism does. It promises to use technology in the building of a "better world." The fanatics of this ideology seem to think that technology alone could do the trick. They seem to believe that democracy is not necessary for progress. Their theories propose the disregarding and even the elimination of both democracy and Christianity.

We cannot but feel tempted to equate these two modern tendencies. The one, namely reactionary materialistic capitalism, stands for not moving at all or even for moving backward. This tendency implies materialism for the

170

sake of class interests. It thinks in terms of private enrichment. The other, revolutionary Marxism, promises to create a "better world"; but when it seizes power it sets out to eliminate democracy and eradicate Christianity. It ends by discarding all moral considerations and limitations. Both tendencies deny spiritual values or pay only lip service to them. Actually they both base their philosophy on sheer materialistic considerations. While the possessors of wealth and power were materialistic in practice, the Marxist revolutionaries professed theoretical materialism. After taking over the government, their practice was also inspired by materialistic self-interest. Both were produced by a soulless, machine age. Both are believers in despiritualized technology. Both are bound to end alike. Both degrade man to a simple means of production. Both think in terms of the leadership by the elite inasmuch as both have a low estimate of the masses. Both look down on the hundreds of millions who, according to them, are unable to direct their own destiny.

Bolshevism is just as dangerous as is unrestricted, uncontrolled capitalism. Both are materialistic, both debase the individual, both flourish in undemocratic societies, and both are indifferent or hostile to Christianity.

2. PERILS OF TECHNOLOGY

Dangers of tragic magnitude lure man on in a technological world which is not safeguarded by democracy and Christianity. The wonderful inventions of our modern age, if misused, can very well cause the destruction of the very society which created them. When no spiritual safeguard exists, when democracy does not fulfill its controlling mission, the time ripens toward dictatorship. Modern dictators are so much more dangerous because—due to modern technology—the technical means for support and maintenance of their rule are so much more effective.

If Christianity is abandoned, if democracy is rejected, power-hungry men who are not responsible to the people, whose action is not limited by any constitutional safeguard against misuse of power, are bound to mis-employ technology. They will misuse technology not only for the sake of perpetuating their egoistic hold over their own enchained people, but they will also use the power they have already built with the help of technology for attacking foreign nations with a view to their ultimate enslavement. There is practically no limit to the potential harmfulness of political power if it is built on the insatiable ambition of men who use the instruments of technology to the limits of their possibility. Thanks to our highly developed technology, it is possible today to reach out for global power and global control. The theoretical limit of man's ambition today reaches the stratosphere. Through technology it has become possible, for good or bad, to control the world from a center. If democracy, which is political responsibility, is eliminated, if the dictatorship of a man or a small group of men is accepted or condoned, then technology is bound to be misused by those who burn with the desire to extend their power to the whole globe.

Technology, when disassociated from democratic control and put in the hands of unscrupulous dictators, can destroy the fruits of the present and of all the past civilizations. Because dictatorship breeds wars, and our modern wars, due to advanced technology, tend to be ever more destructive as they tend to be more global, the stage is set for global destruction. Technology, if democracy disappears from the earth, instead of being the source of general prosperity and peace, could become the instrument of self-destruction.

World wars, which are totalitarian in their use of all the paraphernalia of modern destructive weapons, not only destroy many millions of men, but they also eliminate the possibility of a better life. They bring in their wake mass starvation and all possible kinds of human misery and degradation. The hungry and destitute millions of the world, all participants in the same modern technical civilization, intelligent enough to be aware of the possibility that they too could share in a better, a more prosperous life, are the most fertile soil for ideologies which feed on man's dissatisfaction. World revolutions are the natural consequences of world depressions which in turn are caused, at least partly, by world wars. The false promise of a brotherly world unification to be brought about by the revolt of the millions easily deceives the masses. They sense the utter foolishness of self-motivated and ultimately self-destroying nationalism, which is driving them into "ever better and ever bigger" wars. Having lost spiritual direction in our secularized age, they become the easy prey of an ideology that itself is based on the most materialistic principles.

Technology, misapplied and misused by the masters of the bolshevik empire, became the altar on which the high priests of hatred and self-glorification are unscrupulously sacrificing all the cherished values of human progress. Technology became the base of their power. Technological advance, brought about by sacrificing the interest and freedom of the individual, is said to be the justification for their nefarious actions. Progress, in a technical sense, is offered as an excuse for all the deprivations which they cause to their subjects.

Thus it must be clear that to give up democracy means to give up all the real advantages of technology. But, it

173

means much more. It means betraying progress and turning away from evolution. It means a betrayal of our progressive heritage, a heritage for which man has had to pay so dearly. Elimination of democracy brings irresponsible political leadership. It brings corruption. It brings slow but sure degeneration. It brings shackles for the thinking, thought control, limitation of research, deification of the leader, adoration of those who are in high places. It means physical, intellectual, and spiritual slavery. In such an atmosphere culture begins to rot. Under such reactionary circumstances civilization ceases to advance. Under such conditions man abuses his own talents.

We might think that the best that man can do in such a world is to fossilize the fruits of an age when liberty and democracy still existed. However, fossilization is worse than death. It is the conservation of sin. It is the abuse of life. It is the perpetuation of the criminal instinct of man. It means the extirpation of the divine spark which opens the vistas of progress to man. Fossilization brings death to the soul. It might be better to see a civilization collapse than to witness its fossilization. After the collapse a new start might come in the springtime, but fossilization is holding up the budding of new life.

3. ENDANGERED DEMOCRACY

If technology is based on democracy, if it cannot support itself and bring good fruits in a non-democratic atmosphere, neither can democracy exist without Christianity, which conditions democracy. Democracy grew up in a Christian tradition. While we never can become fully perfect in our behavior, the divine inspiration of Christianity does not touch us without imprinting deep marks upon us. Man never will be able to comprehend the full meaning of the divine life. Still the spark ignited by God was so quickening that it gave a new turn to man's existence. The miracle of this most supreme inspiration was bound to change the meaning of life. It will glow forever.

True, we have applied some of the political implications of Christianity; but many remain to be applied. We know of many implied political commands of Christianity which up to now we have failed to obey. What is more, we are deeply convinced that beyond the inspirations which are carried into life, and beyond the inspirations which some of us sense but most of us ignore, there are in the radiant treasure-house of Christianity innumerable social and political implications of which nobody can yet be aware. They will touch our minds when they are needed. They will be conceived by man in due time. When new problems require new visions for their solution, we will be made capable of discovering them and of using them to our best advantage.

For centuries we have kept our eyes covered and our minds closed. We have not clearly distinguished the political inspirations of Christianity. The treasure of Christianity has been with us for a long time; yet it took many centuries, culminating in the Reformation, to make us aware of some of the commands of Christianity which, when applied, could help us to solve the many problems of human community, together with the fundamental task of setting up the proper universal organization. Who can deny that there must still be many undiscovered and unperceived political implications in Christianity which as yet we can not sense or see?

It is not an accident that ideologies which stand against Christianity are either surreptitiously anti-democratic, or are openly advocates of its elimination. Modern totalitarian ideologies of both types, bolshevik and fascist, when they are in power, are actively engaged in eradicating democracy. They are anti-democratic because they are anti-Christian. They deny the doctrine of the brotherhood of all men. Consequently they are bound to discriminate against groups of men on one ground or another. They deny the doctrine of the divine creation of man. Consequently they deprive man of his God-given human rights. They insult his person and debase his dignity.

Nor does democracy fare much better in those so-called bourgeois countries where godlessness and anti-Christianity loom large or are a permanent menace. They may pretend to stand for democracy, but their resistance against the totalitarian tendencies is undermined by the neglect of or indifference toward the Christian faith. Their democracy is standing on a shaky foundation. This is well illustrated in some west-European countries where democracy is today engaged in a life and death struggle.

Permanency of Christian inspiration is needed if we want to keep on enjoying the fruits of the process of democracy. We cannot expect to see the tree stay alive and ask it to bring forth fruit if we pull its root out of the soil in which it grew. Christianity is needed in order to keep man marching on the road of further democratization. We will miss our way, we will err from our aims, if we throw overboard lightheartedly the compass of Christianity.

As we have asserted several times, progress is a continuous, never-ending process. It means adjustment to the changing times. The progress of democracy is a continuous one, too. We did not reach and never will reach the end of the road. The democratization process is not at its end. Not even political democracy is complete. We do not know what new demands will be brought by the future. However, we know of many problems that are connected with the building of social and economic democracy. For instance, we know that Christianity requires social equality. We know that Christianity postulates the elimination of all human suffering caused by any kind of discrimination. We know that it demands the improvement of the living standard of the millions all over the world. It requires social services; it requires assistance for the fallen and the poor. What is more, Christianity requires the elimination of the greatest economic injustices. While innumerable millions are living near the starvation level, a real Christian cannot enjoy the knowledge that a few are amassing private wealth in staggering quantities.

Loyalty and adherence to Christianity are also needed to extend democracy to all the nations of the globe. Democracy cannot limit itself to a nation. We are not real democrats if the acts of our democracy are confined within the boundaries of our own country. We are not really democrats if we violate the principles of democracy in our relations to our fellow-nations. Peace cannot prevail while the community of nations is adhering to the highly anti-democratic principle of power politics such as is based on force and not on co-operation and consultation. Until this state of affairs in international relations changes, disputes among nations are bound to lead ultimately to wars. International relations, based on power politics, do not recognize the rights of fellow-nations. If they do, they do it only for expediency's sake and only temporarily. They do not recognize equality among nations.

The moral standards as applied to our domestic politics are different from those applied to international relations. Within the frame of the national state, thanks to Christian inspiration, we are on our way toward building democracy even though progress is much endangered by the rise of totalitarian ideology. However, as far as our foreign relations are concerned, we still live in the primitive epoch of the fight of everybody against everybody. This has come about because Christ's spirit has not even touched the surface of our international relations.

We can act democratically in international relations only if we accept the international implications and inspirations of Christianity. We can make the idea of equality among nations work only if we are inspired by the teaching of Christ. We can recognize equal rights for all nations only if we are genuine Christians. Peace can come to this world only if we obey the command of Christ to love one another and to consider each other as brethren. The question of peace is one of trusting each other. We cannot trust each other unless we are convinced that we are brothers who ought to love each other. A new world of peaceful international relations cannot be built unless we accept Christian standards for our dealings with the other nations. Peace can be secured only if democracy can be realized on the international scale.

However, for the present, even national democracy is restricted to only a relatively small part of our globe. Furthermore, even in countries where it is accepted it can not be considered secure. Only certain parts of the Christian West have accepted the principles of political democracy. As far as social and economic democracy are concerned, much remains to be done even where political democracy has been accepted.

The fruits of democracy are not secured, even where they exist today, mostly because anti-democratic forces are rising everywhere on the globe. They are rising because even where political democracy is established it is not implemented with the desirable measure of social and economic democracy. Their challenge is not to be ignored. Because of the progress of technology and science, the interdependence of the different regions of the globe is such that opposing ideologies cannot live alongside each other without clashing. Consequently we have to be engaged in a global crusade for democracy if we want to keep our own democratic form of government.

Democracy is endangered, above all, in our epoch of materialism when its very base, Christianity, is disregarded by the world. Democracy is endangered when influential forces in the West are reluctant to implement fast enough the structure of political democracy which needs progressive measures of social and economic reform. They are retarding the process of building social and economic democracy. Totalitarian ideologies are quick to seize upon this fact, because they thrive on the resulting dissatisfaction of the masses. Democracy is endangered also because it is limited to the confines of the national state and it is not much considered in the relation of nations, though the world in an ideological sense is indivisible.

We did not hide the dangers involved in a politically confused world. However, we firmly believe, as we have stated several times, that the difference between our civilization and the preceding ones is such as to encourage our belief in the coming of a better organized world co-operation. Indeed Christianity, democracy, and technology clearly distinguish our present age. They clearly set our civilization apart. They definitely encourage us to think that we can accomplish what the foregoing generations and ages could not do. World co-operation on the political level is possible today. We certainly could do it with all our advantages. We could do it with the means put into our hands by a benevolent Father. We undoubtedly have a good chance. We ought to do it. But, will we do it?

FINAL WORD

We have finally arrived at the end of the journey. We have based our considerations on the past as it is reflected in the mirror of man's recorded history. We have tried to voice the anguish of an unstable present which is heavy with great expectations but also is loaded with the possibilities of global destruction. We have sensed modern man's hesitation and have expressed the transitional nature of our time. This book was written because, as is natural in times of transition, the question-mark of the future looms large in our soul.

The crucial facts standing out more and more in sharp relief against the background of the gathering storm of a darkened sky and relentlessly imposing themselves for man's consideration are: the oneness of the human race; the fusing of all civilizations; the fact that progress, if it has to, will blast its way into the future; and that modern man could march ahead without the terrible sacrifices of the past.

The means which enable modern man to make intelligent decisions and to take resolute action for avoiding catastrophes of global proportion were also reviewed. The difficulties, dangers, and temptations were not ignored.

What will man do? (Some will prefer to ask: what can he do?)

We found the way well charted, pointing to the goal, towards which the historic forces are driving us today. We do not doubt that this process of final integration can be realized. It might be possible to retard it, but not to hold it up altogether. We should not judge problems of historic importance from the angle of the present impasse. In history even centuries are relatively short. Although unrecorded history reckons in millions of years, recorded history looks back only to five to seven millenniums. Still, looking into the mirror of man's recorded past, we see progressively enlarging political communities. Unless some terrible tragedy should throw us backwards, we cannot be too far (in terms of centuries) from the next international political goal: global integration. We do not doubt, as expressed many times in the pages of this book, what the trend is. The logic of history is so clear that we ought not to misunderstand it. Necessity drives us towards the final integration. No force can resist the tide. The question is rather this: how soon, and how, will the final integration come about?

The big question is whether intelligence, good sense, and logic will play a part in the further integration of mankind or whether we will be the tools of stupid forces beyond our control. The question is whether false prophets, possessed doctrinaires, will drive us, under the pretence of leading us to the right goal, towards the false goal of totalitarianism or whether we will be able to stick to all the achievements of the past: freedom of the mind, liberty of the individual, and political democracy. These principles alone render us capable of reaching the next goal with a minimum of loss and suffering.

Nobody can resist tidal forces. Unification is inevitable because it is necessary; in a material sense it means to adapt our political ways to the necessities of present-day economics and techniques. Bolshevism well understands this necessity. However, its pattern of world unification is retrograde. It recommends and practices the elimination of our Western progressive spiritual heritage, on which the present economic and technologic progress is built and on which also the hope of further political progress is based. One cannot plunge into the building of a new world if one eliminates all the hard-won achievements of the past, which also are necessary to further progress. How could we build a lasting world unit if freedom of the mind, liberty of the individual and political democracy are thrown overboard? The new world, if based on false principles and not on our Christian democratic heritage, would crumble and disappear.

A really new world is bound to rise. But will it be brought about through oceans of spilled blood? Will world revolutions, world wars, and the temporary submerging of all our moral values herald its coming? Will it rise only after political and social earthquakes of unforeseeable magnitude?

Or will we listen to the voice of history and heed the advice of Christianity? Will we be able to avoid all the destructive catastrophes which mark the road through which the fool and the evil pass?

We have observed the logic of history. We believe that there is a road toward progress which avoids catastrophic upheavals. There is a way which does not involve misery, suffering, and destruction. We should have intelligence and we should have faith. Let us stick to the course charted by the proper understanding of history. Let us understand the significance of man's experience. Above all, let us not discard the achievements of the past, for which we have had to pay so dearly. Let us not be the tools of fanatics who base all their calculations on the doctrine of one man.

Faith and intelligence are required. Intelligence comes from understanding history. Faith comes from listening to the message of Christianity.